JUNGZ ANZWER TO JOB UNZIPPED

jOHN ANDREW NOBBS

JOHN ANDREW NOBBS

Copyright © 2018 John Andrew Nobbs

All rights reserved.

ISBN 13: 978-0-9775071-2-2
ISBN 10: 0-9775071-2-2

Frank Theatre Press,
PO Box 7023,
East Brisbane,
Queensland, 4169,
Australia
ABN 52 274 080 202
Email: info@ozfrank.com

DEDICATION

To my long suffering partner

Jacqui Carroll

JOHN ANDREW NOBBS

CONTENTS

Introduction	5
Ch 1 Why William Blake?	11
Ch 2 Precis of Job story	19
Ch 3 Preamble about Jung	25
Ch 4 Jung's background to Job	33
Ch 5 Jung's Preamble to Answer to Job	39
Ch 6 Jung's Answer to Job	51
Jung and the NSP	141

INTRODUCTION

I've been interested in Jung for a number of years since being alerted to the congruency between our film company's performance training and his core beliefs.

I've only studied Jung cursorily, but have been very inspired by his deep interest in the 'unconscious/conscious' psyche dynamic especially with respect to creative endeavours such as acting, dancing and the making of plays, ballets and films.

As our training system developed, I found I was unknowingly using many Jungian precepts in the exercises, and as I read his nifty mini auto bio **Memories, Dreams and Reflections** I found gratifying corroboration for what we were doing in our line of work.

Just as Jung says in his preamble, I'm not trying to 'prove' any of his theories but am using his insights to assist my own searching.

This, my response to Jung's **Answer to Job**, started out as an offset to a film I am aiming to make which documents the building of a ratrod. Because a ratrod build is prosaic I wanted to array it against a theme that was very 'other', and my wife and associate Jacqui Carroll devised a script based on the Job story.

I'll play Job as an Australian welder making a ratrod, which would eventually turn into Leviathon. The idea is to quote chunks of Jung's A to J as I am arcwelding bits of car in a flurry of sparks.. Still to be done, but will in time…

As I perused J's Job book, I became entranced with the revelatory insights that he has brought to bear on the case, but also concerned at how the text was so convoluted and lugubrious…. sorry to say……..Hard to follow! In fact it would take some considerable forensic reading skills to get through his other books, methinks.

With Job he is referring to a known book from the bible, rather than postulating ephemeral possibilities in abstract terms. This gives both Jung and his readers an *articale definite* to hook into, so the theory is applied to something tangible. I think this makes his revelatory insights more easily conveyed.

Not withstanding that, he was history's first and foremost secular surveyor of the soul, with an impressive array of *Conditien Humaine* insights. Rather than hooking into a single smart theory and endlessly trying to prove it like Freud (IMHO), Jung poked in every nook and cranny of the esoteric in the search for what lies behind the mind's door.

So….. does he have to be a great writer as well? No! I figured I'd like to have crack at transcoding **The Answer to Job,** to make it more readable. For, in A to J, he has come up with a map for the devout sceptic - for those like me who seek some sort of divinity, but can't take any clunky religious dogma…

Jung considers that the Book of Job chronicles the seminal event that propitiates the birth of Christ. The book is the odd man out in the Old Testament, in that it reveals God's problematic dark side - problematic for the Christian or Jewish reader, because if 'God is Good' why does he allow bad things to happen to good people?

As such it deliberately paints God in a bad light, and it is surprising that such a critique is even in the bible. Courageous, challenging and maybe long term smart as it furnishes dark ballast for the otherwise 'good' story.

> *If CJ is on the money re the birth of JC,*
> *then surreptitiously the Book of Job is the*
> *Old Testa book that prefigures the New Testa!*

In the A to J there are two subsets of Jung's writing that particularly inspired me: his insights and revelations!

Insights:

By perceptions I mean that he has used his extensive understandings of Mankind's psyche to read between the lines of the text, arriving at some surprising and plausible psychological insights into the interactive God /Job/ mankind drama.

They take the form of a sequence of events starting with the Garden of Eden and culminating in the birth of Christianity:

1. The Fall: Adam and Eve were shown the tree of knowledge by God, who, after forbidding them to eat of it, cast them out of Eden. This shows a very ambivalent God. First of all he shows them the tree… then he tells them not to eat of its knowledge, if they do they will die on the same day.. then kicks them out of the garden…Much confused thinking that was caused by God not wanting man to become conscious (gain wisdom), but Jung argues very plausibly that God didn't want mankind to know (be conscious of) him.

2. Job is forced to use wisdom to deal with God. The first outcome of the Job 'Challenge' is that God triggers Job's consciousness.

3. For the first time God has come up against a human who stands firm in his beliefs.

4. Job effectively 'out goods' (proves himself more righteous than) God. And when God doesn't apologise, but instead launches into a pyroclastic diatribe on Job's obvious and self acknowledged insignificance, God shows fault, a fissure in his otherwise perfection. With that, Job sees to the back of God's mind, and unwittingly has come to know God.

5. This imperfection means that God has to reinvent himself, and the only way he can do that is come back in human form.

6. Jung makes the observation that after Job, there are no more covenants, no more attempts to re-contract the relationship with man. In an almost admittance of his misbehaviour, God decides unilaterally to re-incarnate himself.

7. Satan appears as an existent force in the bible for the first time in the book of Job, and Jung reckons that after the birth of Christ, the dark one's role is considerably diminished.

Jung arrived at these astute positions by reading the bible, neither as a book of faith, nor a book of fact, but as a document that outlines mankind's search for union (fulfilment) with God.

Revelations:

By revelations I mean he has lit on two direct statements from the New Testament and discovered some truly profound meanings that have been normally missed. Such as:

1. In the Lord's Prayer, there is a section:

   "Lead us not into temptation, but deliver us from evil"

   The second part is a straightforward plea for assistance, but… look at the first line! Jesus is saying to God, his father: "Do not tempt people to to bad things." That is in itself immoral! Jung says that Jesus is imploring God not to go back to his old habits, e.g. Tree of Knowledge duplicity, but more of that later!

2. When Jesus is about to expire on the cross, he utters the famous last words:

   "My God, my God, why hast thou forsaken me?"

Jung has a perceptive take on this too, in the body of Answer to Job.

I've taken two inspirational points from these Jung revelations; one is the revelations themselves and the corollary: The bible can be construed from a position that is halfway between fact and fiction- what Jung would call a 'Psychic Fact'

As a follow on, the existence of such poetic material in a universal document as influential and as studied as the Bible means that said material has been accepted as part of the Godzone by generations of people, who at least respect and, more often, revere its spiritual import.

Jung's acute revelations of inform his Answer to Job and confer a type of archetypical authority if one considers that they havbeen accepted by many people in many societies as written portraits of divine experience (what Jung calls Collective Unconscious).

> *Spurred on by Jung's example I have a revelation of my own with reference to the expulsion from the Garden of Eden:*
>
> *Genesis 2: 17: "but of the tree of the knowledge of good and evil, thou shalt not eat of it, for in the day that thou eatest thereof, thou shalt surely die…."*
>
> *What gives? Was God telling porkies, or should Adam and Eve have read it as a metaphysical death?*

In my work, I have been inspired by many of Jung's discoveries such as archetypes and the uncon/con, to view the bible, not as God's word, or historical fact, but as a progressive work of art that portrays mankind's search for Godzone.

The Bible itself is the final chapter of a multi-millennial search, that started with trogs in caves, and gradually evolved in tandem with developments in technology. The New Testament being the dernier cri of Godzone, deconstructed by the Steel and Steam of the first industrial revolution and finally obliterated by the discovery of the atom, and the liturgy of Quantum Mechanics.

CHAPTER 1 : WHY WILLIAM BLAKE ?

William Blake , esq, Londoner, 1787- 1827

Jung began to study Blake seriously in 1948 and came to the conclusion that in dealing with archetypal/mythological material, Willy was the real deal. Blake's poetry and painting demonstrates Jung in so many ways, especially the Uncon of Innocence and the Con of Experience.

Since my late teens I have been fascinated by the mystical poet and painter that was William Blake (1787-1827). He was, like Jung, keenly interested in the Job story and did a suite of drawings based on it, which I'm using for the pics in the main body of the text.

In many ways his artistic mind was a good match for Jung's Con/Uncon dialectical explanations, and since Jung provided no visual clues I've used other Blake drawings to pepper the text.

One hundred years before quantum mechanics, his art both in word and on canvas was born of what he called 'contraries' which is really another name for wave /particle duality(**WPD**)!

THE THEME OF WAVE/PARTICLE PARADOX

Here I must articulate what I mean by wave/particle duality,(WPD) an epigram I'll use thoughout this book. Its an admittedly simplistic mental equation that I use to interconnect many aspects of artistic thinking/feeling processes in artistic pursuits.

In this book it conjoins the art and poetry of Mystic Blake, the insights of Scholar Jung and the analysis of Brainiac Einstein and others - I did say it was simplistic!

Scientifically it was the key to apprehending the contradictory nature of light. Light behaves as both a wave (that's how it can travel through empty space), and at the same time is also a particle (that's how it gets bent as it goes around things....., e.g. Moon looks bigger at moonrise).

It was impossible to resolve these two supposed opposites until Albert E. used his unconscious mind to get between blob and ripple and suck 'em together.

Once sorted it was go, go, go for the entire kingdom of for electro-magnetism, paving the way for the electronic revolution of C20.

This same paradox can be transposed to Jung's Con /Uncon for differentiating the psyche, Blake's Contraries for his mystical Art and Poetry, and Jung's way of reading the Book of Job.

There are several instances in his 'Answer to Job' where Carl invokes the WPD..... and I'll point them out as we go.....

He termed them 'innocence' and 'experience', and went beyond a simplistic oppositionism of good/bad to a compound dialectic of light and dark.

Innocent poems like:

> "**Little lamb, who made thee,
> dost thou know who made thee….**"

Are balanced by the 'experience' poems like:

> "**Tyger, Tyger Burning bright,
> In the forests of the night…**"

The tyger is not evil, so much as an elemental mysterious force of nature, which cannot be tamed or understood, only feared and accepted.

He brings the worlds of innocence and experience together in the last stanza of 'Tyger':

> **"When the stars threw down their spears,**
> **And watered heaven with their tears,**
> **Did he smile his work to see,**
> **Did he who made the lamb, make thee…"**

Jung began to study Blake seriously in 1948 and came to the conclusion that he was dealing with archetypal/mythological material. In terms of the 'individuation' process Blake is more Jungian than Jung!

Blake's poetry and painting demonstrates Jung in so many ways , especially the Uncon of Innocence and the Con of Experience.

In his painting, he was capable of some very stretched and psychedelic thinking. He was once talking to a friend in his parlour when he left off and said: "Hold it! I've just seen the ghost of a flea!"

He stopped everything else and proceeded to draw and then paint it. The result was an extraordinary painting, a sort of 'The Creature of the Black Lagoon' - the type of image that would have been pretty off-the-wall even in 1989 let alone in 1819.

And he wasn't trying to be smart or scare people-he just said he painted what he imagined, what he saw in his mind.

He always maintained that he painted or wrote what was in his imagination, and anyone and everyone had the same capability if they were prepared to foster it.

WB's Ghost of a Flea (100 yrs before Dali, etc)

Both of those answers are pretty lucid and logical, certainly linear enough to not be those of a madman, of which he was often accused. They also show that his Conscious was calmly aware of what his Unconscious was doing. A very good parallel of the way Jung calmly navigates the middle ground between the 'fact' and 'fiction' of the Bible.

Blake's whole life's quest was to portray his search, to create a document in poetry and painting that would be the outward illustration of his highly idiosyncratic inner journey. His paintings and poetry are a road map and diary of, what Jung would call, his God Impulse-his spirit's search for an auto-gnostic godhead.

The sort of Blake painting that would do Francis Bacon proud 120 years later!

He would today be called a revolutionary Christian, because he held views that paralleled Christ's 'money changers in the temple' fracas. Combine that with a Francis of Assisi style pacifism, and you have a very progressive cat, way ahead of his time.

One of the reasons Blake is so central to this book, is that his poetry and painting represented the actualisation of so many things that Jung TALKED about! I put this book together because I am intensely interested and inspired by Jung's ideas, but find his writings contorted.

I hadn't reckoned that Carl himself was capable of some pretty good art, until I got my hands on the massive BIG RED BOOK.

The BRB is full of mandalas that he drew as 'pictograms of the soul'. Many of them like the pic below embody a far more elastic depth of field than your standard 'crafty' mandala. But, like others of his ilk, they talk about artists like they are different human beings-specimens as it were..........which I find a bit odd.

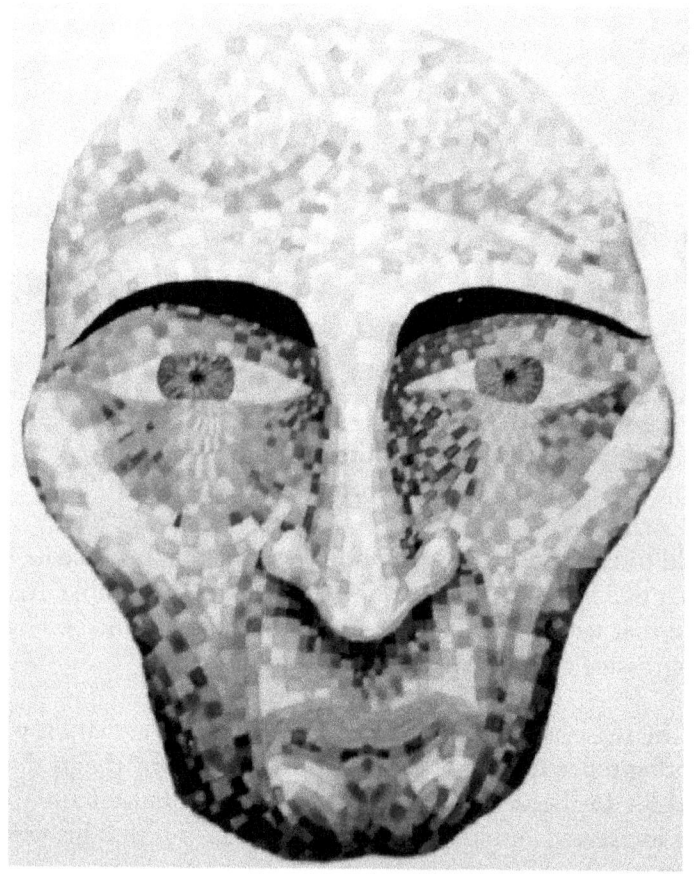

Pretty Spooky pic that comes out of Carlo's own 40 days in the wilderness

CHAPTER 2: PRECIS OF JOB'S STORY

Job is an all round good guy, and he has kids, a wife, land, and a bunch of pastoralised animals. Doesn't get much better than that. Up in the heavens, God brags to the divine assembly about Job. Lo and behold, Satan pipes up and challenges God on Job's goodness.

What We Know About Satan

Satan looking pretty suave, having pulled a swifty over Eve.

This is not the cartoon Satan with horns and pointy tail. In Hebrew, Satan actually means "The Accuser" so one might see him as a provocateur. He appears in the bible for the first time in Job and only features in Chapters 1 and 2.

> **Aspects of Satan to Consider**
>
> *(1) Satan spends a good amount of time down on earth. When God asks him where he's been, Satan always replies that he's been hanging out on earth. All Angels, good and bad, get to do that.*
>
> *(2) He isn't a pushover. Satan challenges God not once, but twice. So God takes him seriously and in fact God treats him like a wayward son-gives him a lot of lattitude.*
>
> *(3) He's pretty powerful. Remember, God doesn't inflict anything nasty on Job with his own divine power. Instead, he allows Satan to use his own uber pranks, then conveniently forgets the bad boy was ever at it.*

Back to the story. Satan tells God that, sure, Job loves God now, but take away his earthly possessions and his children, and he will dump God in a flash. God doesn't like this but instead of dissing Satan, he takes the bait.

He agrees to the challenge, and Satan unleashes a force that kills all of Job's family and his servants, assorted livestock, and reduces all his possessions to dust. He loses everything, except for his wife, who only appears to be still there so she can nag him.

But guess what? Job remains loyal. He complains alright, but refuses to denounce God. Take that, Satan. God goes back to bragging and Satan sets up another challenge.

This time, God lets Satan afflict Job with rashes, boils, and blisters all over his body But not to dispatch him! That would be pretty pointless, and hardly a lesson if he's not alive to get it- but also raises another very important point (more of which later).

Now Job becomes a much less happy camper.

After all, he was loyal to God, and look what happened. He doesn't renounce God, but he does insist that he at least deserves some kind of explanation. His buddies Eliphaz, Bildad, and Zophar aren't much help because they suggest it was Job's own fault. Hmmm…. with friends like these….

Job isn't quite satisfied with that explanation. Just in the nick of time, another mate Elihu pops in to tell Job that he may not have sinned, but he still has no right to question his fate. After all, God's universe is still endowed with immortal power. Bottom line: get used to it!.

But! Our man will not crack! Still complains but will not curse God.

After figuring that Job won't crack, God finally shows up, appearing out of a whirlwind, no less. Why? Not to apologise, but for an almighty vituperative demonstration of cosmic power and indignity.

"Where was Job on the day the universe was created? Where was Job when God was designing the architecture of the seas and the continents? Where was Job when God, etc, etc?"

Needless to say, Job feels even more humbled and acknowledges that, as a mere mortal, he can't possibly understand everything in an immortally ruled universe. Taking Elihu's advice, Job continues to cop it sweet, and eventually God gives him double what he had at the outset.

Job's Wife

When Satan does the dirty deeds on Job, for some reason Job's wife survives. Obviously to give him an ear full:

> **"Do you still persist in your integrity?**
> **Curse God, and die!"**

Job avoiding wife's entreating gaze

Hmmm. Sounds a bit waspishly predictable, but that's just it. Misery and death often go hand in hand, and Job's wife is there to remind us of just that. Job, of course, responds like a hen pecked husband:

"You speak as any foolish woman would speak. Shall we receive the good at the hand of God, and not receive the bad?"

Back To the Beginning again. All for what?

By the very end of the story, Mrs. Job seems to bear her husband a bunch of kids, of which capriciously, only the girls are mentioned. All the way back to square one!

Job lives to a ripe old age, and both God and Satan leave him alone.

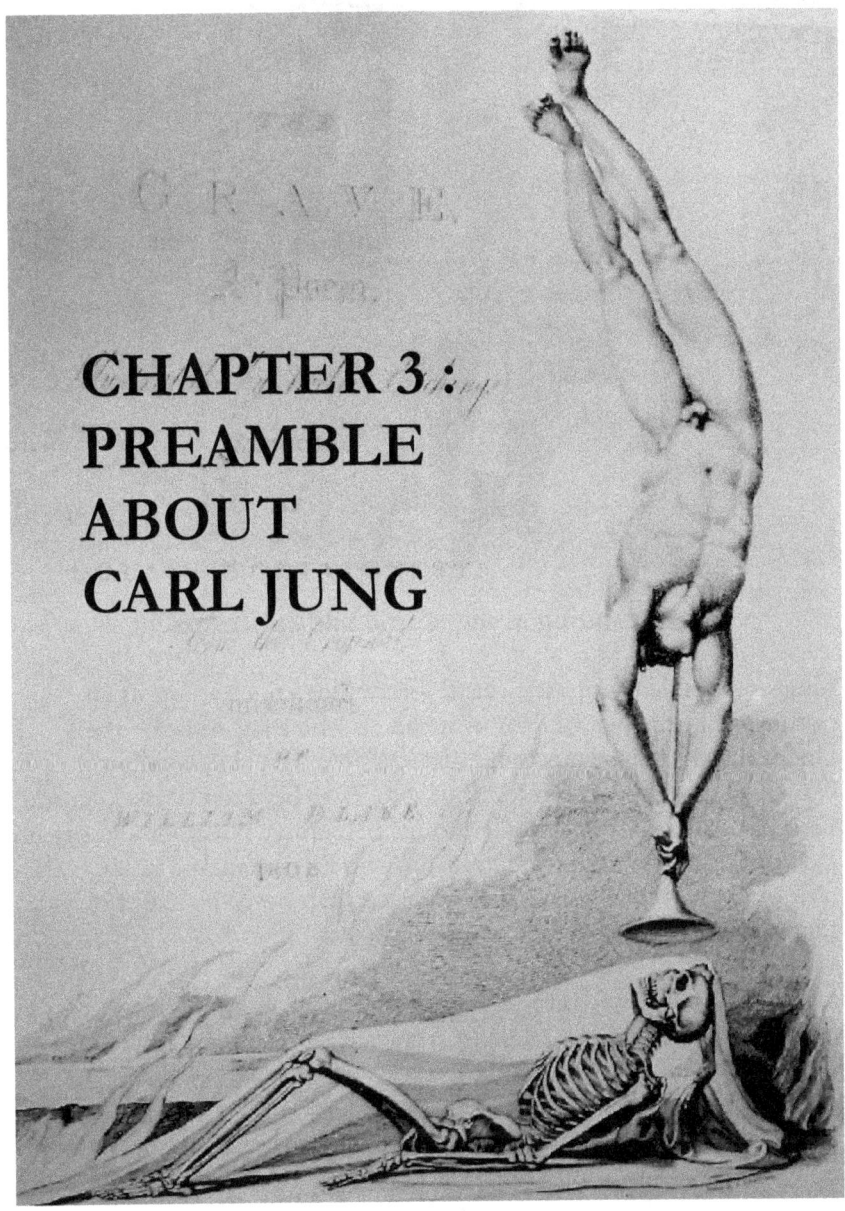

CHAPTER 3: PREAMBLE ABOUT CARL JUNG

Jung Brooding at the family pile at Khusnacht

Jung's preamble to the Answer to job outlines the lead up to his putting pen to paper, but for us it can also be a key to using the Unconscious/Conscious mind dialectic that he did so much to explore. It was his deep interest in the offset between Conscious and Unconscious processes that led to his perceptive interrogation of the Book of Job. As a by product, he has shown us a third (lateral) way to look at the bible, less easily dismissed than both the Truth or Fiction oppositional viewpoints.

Most people read the bible either as a book of fact, or, on the opposite side, as a book of faith. Typically, either side flatly rejects the opposing view..

Jung steers down the middle, using a dualist approach that is half way between fact and feeling. Whether he did this consciously or unconsciously (I suspect the latter!), he is invoking the classic wave/ particle conceivings of Quantum

Mechanics in order to deal with the paradoxical duality of God. Scientists such as Einstein used wave particle duality to come to an understanding as to how light actually worked and the reference is wonderfully apposite, because so often is Light mentioned as a metaphor for God.

Jung's DIY hideyhole at Bollingen from the lake

His 'third' way is summed up in his use of the term: 'Psychic Facts':

" Some people believe it to be physically true that Christ was born as the son of a virgin, but others deny this as a physical impossibility. Beliefs of this kind are psychic facts which cannot be contested and need no proof. Religious statements refer to things that cannot be established as physical facts. The psyche is an autonomous Zone, and religious statements are psychic confessions which are based on unconscious, i.e. on transcendental, processes."

(Transcendental means relating to a spiritual realm)

Jung appears to be wary of letting us know how he views God, and only gives one hint as far as I can find in the A to J, that nevertheless cleaves between fact and feeling:

"After all, we can imagine God as an internally flowing current of vital energy that endlessly changes shape, just as easily as we can imagine him as an eternally unmoved, unchanging essence."

Jung's really cool barrel vaulted study at Bollingen

It is compelling that Jung here is conceiving his God in terms of Quantum wave/particle duality even so far as using a 'wave' term like river, and 'particle' terms like unchanging essence. This is very intuitive, in that Godhead in all its guises is an agglomeration of paradoxes, and wave particle thinking is a most perceptive way to address its compound nature.

In fact the Book of Job is the one book in the bible that faces the good/bad paradox of God.

The build up of Godzone leading to Job

Jung gives a short heads up on the development of mankind's delineation of God (what I precociously call Godzone) as a projection of people's collective desire for spiritual satisfaction. He sees it as a process evolving over millennia, citing a few epochs as examples which I've re-summarised as:

1. Pagan animism for no tech, low literacy cultures - 'Spirit of the rock' - No anthropomorphism….

2. More advanced metallurgic and agricultura cultures, e.g. Egyptian pantheism of place and discrete function-semi anthropomorphic (Gods with animal heads and human bodies)…..

3. The fully anthropomorphic God of the bible, whose spirit is everywhere/all the time…..

Jung maintained that A to J was his only book with which he felt happy, probably because he had the 'ne plus ultra' Godzone archetype on which to hang his hat.

In his theoretical landscape an Archetype is:
> A primitive mental image inherited from the earliest human ancestors, and supposed to be present in the collective unconscious. (Wikipedia)

The God of Christianity must be the big Kahuna of Archetypes, because it has dominated word, thought and deed for millennia. Starting off as an offspring of the Jewish religion, Christianity is the only mainstream religion that has redefined itself in tandem with evolving technology.

No hot and cold running here! CJ pumping away

If one gauges the increasingly anthropomorphic correlation between God and Man through the ages, the familial bond has grown in parallel with Mankind's increasing control of the physical materia of the natural world.

As mankind's mastery of technology has allowed a more symbiotic relationship with the physical world, this has enabled a more advanced spiritual and poetic attitude towards nature itself.

With, paradoxically, a corresponding drop off in the poetic depiction of God! My guess is that in the days of John Donne, et al. the populace was terrified of God, because life was nasty, brutish and short! Men had almost no control over health and well being, the precariousness of which they attributed to God's caprices……

Furthermore, most people would have felt they were always on the cusp of meeting Him pretty soon - death was always close!. Therefore their poetry was very respectful and full of propitiating praise.

Steel, Steam and Poetry

A good example of this 'advanced spiritual and poetic attitude' is the Western poetry that celebrates the spiritual love of nature only really began with the industrial revolution-the knowledge and application of steel and steam.

Quite different in the East, where their more accepting attitude to life's slings and arrows allowed a more phlegmatic writing of poetry about nature. By the same token, when the west got around to it, their strident new found appreciation of nature led to a much more scintillating poetry….

Before the advent of Steam and Rail, mountains were not poetic, they were barriers-travel was long and arduous! But the ability to bore through a mountain, meant that they became enjoyable, and their spiritual attributes could be lauded.

Gnomic glyphs rock hewn by Jung at Bollingen

This technological tempering of nature as more benign paralleled the Godzone, where advanced Christian communities such as Protestants conceived a more equal compact with their God. The dropping of the draconian 'Original Sin', and the obviating of the Confessional, meant that your layman had more responsibility written into the contract, making the anthropomorphic to and fro even more symbiotic.

There's another filament to this thread; the industrial revolution also prepared the ground for the scientific discovery of evolution, which killed the idea of God as a bearded old guy with big hands. This led to huge ructions in the religious academia, where there was in the late nineteenth century a flurry of soul searching around the choice between Anglican and Catholic. This angst ridden void created by Darwin and his ilk was eventually filled by Psychiatry, and this is where our man Jung comes in - being Swiss and Lutheran, this is pretty much Jung's turf.

CHAPTER 4:

JUNG'S BACKGROUND TO JOB

rewritten by

John Andrew Nobbs

Some Godzone backgrounding leading up to the Book of Job in Jung's words:

How the people of the old Testament felt about their God we know from the testimony of the Bible.

The powerful personality of Yahweh had raised him above all the gods of place of the Gentiles and had immunised him against the influence that for several centuries have been undermining the authority of the pagan gods.

Mankind had found the stories around the pagan gods more and more incomprehensible and absurd. Yahweh, however, had no origin and no past, except his creation of the world, with which all history began. Add to this his relation to that part of mankind whose forefather Adam he had fashioned in his own image as the original man, by what appears to have been a special act of creation.

Of course one must not tax an archaic God with the attitudes of modern ethics. For the people of early Antiquity things were rather different.

In their gods there was absolutely everything: they teemed with virtues and vices. Hence they could be punished, put in chains, deceived, stirred up against one another without losing face, or at least not for long.

The man of that epoch was so inured to divine inconsistencies that he was not unduly perturbed when they happened.

For the Jews (or the Israelites as they were then known) such divine inconsistencies of multiple Gods became aggregated into one being, Yahweh. He was an agglomeration of paradoxes- an **Antinomy**.

(Antinomy: a contradiction between two beliefs or conclusions that are in themselves reasonable.)

Amongst many other self-contradictions, this being, Yahweh, proved to be a jealous defender of morality, even though he himself was amoral.

He was especially sensitive in regard to justice. Hence he had always to be praised as 'just', which it seemed was very important to him. He made pressing demands on his people to be praised and propitiated in every possible way.

The character that's revealed fits a personality who is defined by his relationship to an external object. Such dependence on the object becomes absolute when the subject is totally lacking in self-reflection (consciousness) and therefore has no insight into himself.

Yahweh shows that he is not really conscious of himself, otherwise he would put an end to the unnecessary **Panegyrics** (overweening praise) he is seeking for his 'justice'.

That is why the Creator needs conscious man as a type of witness even though, he would like to prevent man from becoming conscious. And that is also why Yahweh needs the acclamation of a small group of people (the Jews).

Thanks to this need for recognition, he had a distinct personality, which differed from that of an archaic king only in scope. His jealous and irritable nature, prying mistrustfully into the faithless hearts of men and exploring their secret thoughts, compelled a personal relationship between himself and man, who then could not help but be sucked into God's emotionally charged discordancies.

That was the essential difference between Yahweh and the Hellenic equivalent Zeus, who in a benevolent and somewhat detached manner allowed the universe to roll along on it's accustomed course and punished only those who misbehaved.

He did not moralise but ruled purely instinctively. He did not demand anything more from human beings than the sacrifices due to him and had no plans for them. Father Zeus is certainly an authority but but with no real emotional character or psychological dimension.

Yahweh, on the other hand, was interested in man. Humans were of the highest importance to him. He needed them as they needed him, urgently and primally. Zeus too could throw thunderbolts about but only at hopelessly disorderly individuals. Against mankind as a whole he had no objections—but then they didn't interest him all that much.

Yahweh, however, could get inordinately excited about man as a species and men as individuals if they did not behave as he desired or expected, without ever considering that in his omnipotence, he could easily have created something better then these "bad earthenware pots."

His intense nature, prying into the hearts of men and exploring their secret thoughts, compelled a personal relationship between himself and mankind, who could not help but feel emotionally called by him.

In view of this intense personal relatedness to his chosen people, it was only to be expected that a regular covenant would develop which also extended to certain individuals, for instance, to David. As we learn from the 89th Psalm, Yahweh told him:

> **"My steadfast love I'll keep for him for ever,**
> **And my covenant will stand firm for him.**
> **I will not violate my covenant, or alter the word**
> **that went forth from my lips. Once for all I have**
> **sworn by my holiness; I will not lie to David."**

Yet it happened that Yahweh, who watched so jealously over the fulfilment of laws and contacts, broke his own oath.

The man of that epoch was so inured to other divine inconsistencies that he was not unduly perturbed when they happened. With Yahweh the case was different because, from quite early on, the familial and moral tie began to play an important role in the religious relationship. In these circumstances a breach of contract was bound to have the effect not only of a personal but of a moral injury.

One can see it from the way David answers Yahweh:

> "How long, Lord?
> Wilt thou hide thyself forever?
> Shall thy wrath burn like fire?
> Remember how short my time is:
> Wherefore has thou made all men in vain?"
> ....
> "Lord, where are the former loving kindnesses,
> Which by thy faithfulness thou didst swear to David?"

Had this been addressed to a human being it would have run something like this:

"For heaven's sake, man, pull yourself together and stop being such a senseless Savage! It is really too grotesque to get into such a rage when it's partly your own fault that the plants wont flourish. You used to be quite reasonable and took good care of the garden you planted, instead of trampling it to pieces"

With God's suspiciousness the mere possibility of doubt was enough to infuriate him and induce that peculiar double-faced behaviour of which he had already given proof in the Garden of Eden, when he pointed out the tree to the First Parents and at the same time forbad them to eat it. In this way he precipitated the fall, which he apparently never intended.

The special providence which singled out the Jews from among the rest of humanity and made them the "chosen people" had burdened them from the start with a heavy obligation. As usually happens with such mortgages, they quite understandably tried to circumvent it as much as possible.

Since the chosen people used every opportunity to break away from him, and Yahweh felt it of vital importance to tie this indispensable tribe indefinitely to himself, he proposed to the patriarch Noah a contract between himself on the one hand, and Noah, his children, and all their animals, on the other.

In order to give compassionate meaning to this contract, he instituted the rainbow as a token of the covenant. If, in the future, he summoned the thunderclouds which hide within them floods and lightning, then the rainbow would appear, reminding Noah and his people of the benefits.

In spite of of such precautions the contract had gone to pieces with David, an event which left behind it literary deposits in the Scriptures at which grieved some few of the devout. The fatal impression made by the breach-of-contract survived. It is historically possible that these considerations influenced the author of the book of Job.

CHAPTER 5:

JUNG'S PREAMBLE TO
JOB

rewritten by
John Andrew Nobbs

The suggestion that I should tell you how **Answer to Job** came to be written sets me a difficult task, because the history of my response to the Book of Job can barely be told in a few words. I have been fascinated by its central theme for years. Different sources nourished the evolution of my attitude, until one day, and after long reflection, the time was right (1952). The most immediate cause of my writing the book is perhaps to be found in certain issues I raised in my book Aion.

> ### Aion (1951)
>
> *Much in this volume is concerned with the evolution of Christianity and and with the figure of Christ. Jung explores how Christianity came into being when it did, the importance of Christ as a symbolic figure and the identification of that figure with the archetype of the Self. The book discusses the problem of opposites, particularly good and evil (From Wiki).*

In connection with the discussion of these paradoxes, I outlined the problematic nature of *privatio boni* (the Absence of Good). To whit, if we postulate the existence of an absolute concept of "good", it must needs be balanced by its opposite, an equally substantial "bad" or "evil". If "good" and "evil" exist as absolute and eternal, they cannot be attributed to man, since "God the good" and "Satan the evil one" existed before man as co-existent opposites.

If Christianity claims to be a Monotheism, it is an automatic assumption that such opposites as Good and Evil are contained and united in God.

This has been established because throughout the bible Satan is considered to an aspect of God, i.e. he is often referred to as one of the "Sons of God".

JUNGZ ANZWER TO JOB UNZIPPED

This problematic dialectic of the 'Good and Bad conjoined in God' is most vividly portrayed in the Book of Job, for Job himself expected help from God against God - i.e he hoped to utilise the good grace of God to countermand God's bad tendencies. Job's story completely encapsulates the issues of the opposites in God the *complexio oppositorium*.

Over the years, numerous questions, not only from my patients, but from all over the world, pressured me to give a more complete and explicit answer that I had given in **Aion**.

For quite some time I hesitated to do this because I knew what a storm would be raised. But eventually I was so gripped by the revelatory value of the Book of Job that I was unable to ignore it - therefore I found myself obliged to deal with the whole story, and I did so in the form of describing my personal attitude, driven by a purely subjective point of view.

I deliberately chose this form because I wanted to avoid the impression that I had any intention of announcing an "Eternal Truth". The book does not pretend to be any more than the voice of an individual who hopes and expects to meet with thoughtful responses from the public.

> *JAN: In this last sentence, CJ is obviously expecting a firestorm of controversy to descend on him given the overly conservative culture of the early 50's when the booklet was first published. Wisely, he ducked for cover under 'personal' tag, and raised the pow wow flag hoping for 'thoughtful response'.*

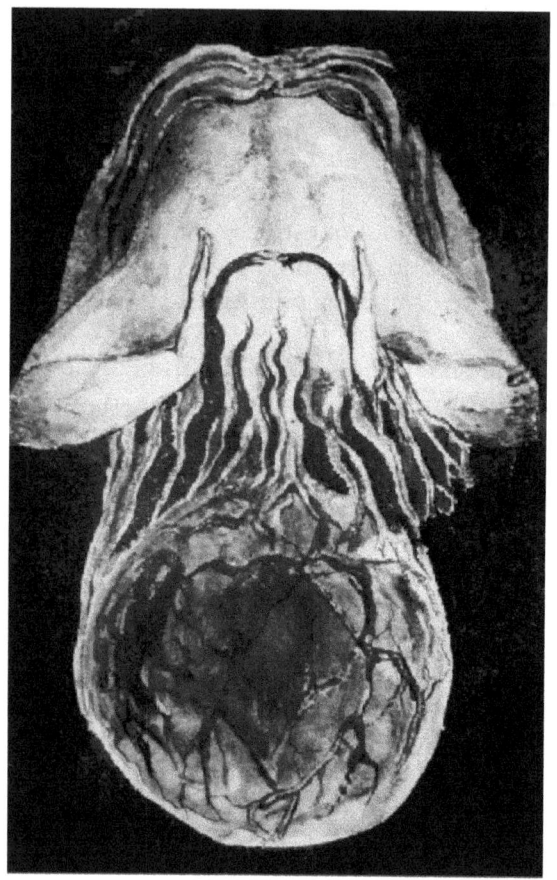

Willy pic that could be early space Hubble telescope

Preface:

On account of its somewhat provocative content, my little book requires a short preface. I beg of you, dear reader, not to overlook it. For in what follows, I shall speak of things concerning the sacrosanct nature of religious belief. Whoever challenges holy matters inevitably runs the risk of being torn to pieces by the two parties who are in emotionally charged conflict about their imputation. This conflict is due to the strange supposition that a thing is true only if it presents itself as a provable physical fact.

Psychic facts

Thus some people believe it to be physically true that Christ was born as the son of a virgin, but others deny this as a physical absurdity. Everyone can see that there is no emotional solution to this 'faith vs science' conflict. Both are right and both are wrong. Yet they could easily reach agreement if only they replaced the word physical.

"Physical" is not the only criterion of truth: there are also psychic truths which can neither be explained or proved nor contested in any physical way. If, for instance, a general belief existed that the River Rhine had at one time flowed backwards from its mouth to its source, then this belief in itself would be a fact even though such an assertion, from a pure scientific standpoint, would be deemed utterly absurd.

Beliefs of this kind are **psychic facts** and religious conceptions are of this type. They refer to things that cannot be provable as physical facts. In terms of anything physically 'real', they make no logical sense and science would dismiss them as non-credible - mere 'magical mysterious' miracles.

The fact that religious phenomena are unprovable does not lessen their value, but demonstrates that in contrast to physical perception the domain of the spirit has its own 'qualitative' value system, which is unable to be critiqued by using 'quantifiable' physical data.

This autonomy (self governance) implies that religious phenomena are to be regarded not only as independent objects but also as subjects with laws of their own. From a rational point of view, we can, of course, describe them dispassionately as objects, and even explain them up to a point.

But we are also compelled to treat them as stand alone subjects which may be powerfully effective but difficult to quantify after. In other words, we have to admit that they possess passionate belief and moral purpose, and a kind of unconscious free will.

> *JAN: This is another example of Jung's intuitive Wave /Particle (W/P) perceptions. It is fascinating that he never directly mentions any Quantum Physics analogies, at least in Answer to Job, but his whole discussion is informed by them.*
>
> *It is a fascinating demonstration of his own theories on Synchronicity, that W/P 'thought experiments' as used by Einstein from 1905 are synchronous with Jung's developing career.....*

The unconscious part of the psyche is an **autonomous** zone, and religious statements represent some of the manifestos emanating from the psyche. Such manifestos and the like are driven by the unconscious, i.e. on processes which cause effects which are profound but often veiled and difficult, if not impossible, to quantify.

The best and most obvious example of the psychic manifestos driven by unconscious processes are dreams. Dreams are a type of audio/visual portrait of the turbid sub-liminal workings of the mind.

They then influence our external behaviour as they apply pressure to the conscious part of the brain: this can be gradual or sudden depending on many factors, but suffice it to say that they often manifest as 'inexplicable' or surprising day to day actions.

Definition of Autonomous:

By autonomous Carl means governed by its own set of forces, not so much 'rules' in the way that the conscious part of the brain works, but a chain of stimulae that enact behaviour which is rationally inexplicable.

JAN: A quick take on Conscious/Unconscious

The Unconscious consists of the processes in the mind which occur automatically and are not available to introspection, and include thoughts, memories, interests, and motivations. Even though these processes exist well under the surface of conscious awareness they exert an impact on behaviour that is in ways difficult to measure.

The term was coined by the 18th-century German Romantic philosopher Friedrich Schelling, but most well known in the work of Freud and Jung. The Unconscious should be considered as the obverse of the Conscious mind, which is the part of the brain which deals in rational thoughts and actions. In simplistic terms the Conscious deals in 'facts' such as life saving and sustaining processes, while the Uncon deals in 'feelings' such as dreams, wishes, hopes.

By using the terms 'obverse' and 'converse' parts of the mind (much like obverse and converse sides of a coin), the con and uncon can be shown as interdependent but separate aspects of the brain...

It has been said that if the mind can be seen as an iceberg, the conscious part is that above water, and the uncon below.

It can also be said that the Conscious is responsible for the sustaining of life, but the unconscious IS life!

That is why whenever I speak of religious experiences, I am in a world of images and symbols that point to something **ineffable** *(too great or extreme to be expressed or described in words)*.

It is difficult (if not impossible) to know how clear or unclear these images and symbols are, in respect to the transcendental experience to which they point.

If, for instance, I use the word "God", I give expression to a verbal symbol which has undergone much evolution in the course of mankind's history, creating a panorama of images and ideas which are products of both human imagination and temporal and parochial concerns.

I am, however, unable to say with any degree of certainty – unless it be by faith – whether these changes affect only the images and concepts, or have changed the unspeakable itself.

There is no doubt that there is something behind these images that transcends consciousness because all societies have felt these **numinous** (having a strong religious or spiritual quality) urges, and created portraits that range from the Stone Age paintings at Lascaux to Salvador Dali. Surprisingly, these have developed in such a way that the iconography does not vary limitlessly and chaotically, but in all cases they reduce to a few basic principles or archetypes.

This imagery, like the psyche itself, is unknowable and unprovable as such. Such symbols are inadequate and only representational and, for a numinous experience, can only be felt.

But, although our whole world of religious ideas consists of anthropomorphic images that could never stand up to scientific scrutiny, we should never forget that they are based on numinous archetypes, i.e., on unconscious projections which are unassailable by reason. We are dealing with psychic facts which logic can ignore but not supplant.

Tertullian (*155 -240 AD The first Christian author to produce an extensive corpus of Latin Christian literature. He has been called 'the founder of Western theology.'*)

In this context Tertullian described the testimony of the soul.

In his **De Testimonio Animae,** he says:

"These testimonies of the soul are as simple as they are true, as common as they are obvious, as natural as they are common, as divine as they are natural. I think they cannot appear to anyone to be trifling and ridiculous if one considers the majesty of Nature, whence the authority of the soul is derived......."

I would go a step further and say that the statements made by people in the Holy Scriptures are also utterances of the soul, because they are unconscious projections.

The conscious mind makes statements that may easily be snares, delusions, lies, or arbitrary opinions because they are deliberate expressions of the will or Ego.

This is not true of the statements of the soul for they are statements of spiritual desire or search: they point to experiences that exceed daily thinking. These experiences are types of **entia** (*an actual thing, as distinct from a quality or characteristic*) which are the archetypes, projections of mankind's collective unconscious, and which have appeared in the form of mythological motifs over millennia.

Archetypes exist as eternal symbols of mankind's unconscious impulses, and as such, are never invented, but enter and leave the mind's instinctive perception as finished insights, for instance in dreams.

> *JAN: Archetype: a collectively inherited unconscious idea, pattern of thought, image, etc. Here's a modern version of an archetype:*
> *Think Dirty Harry wearing stove pipe trousers, cuban heeled boots on the railway line .. Gothic black nemesis!*
>
> *We were in the backblocks of Pakistan, saw a bunch of villagers glued to an old TV... couldnt take their eyes off him!*
>
> *To me that image would be an archetype, because it transcends the time and place it was made, such that it has an equivalent impact twenty thousand miles away twenty years later...*
>
> *For my money, Archetypes are the best idea that Jung ever hooked into. Not sure if he invented them, but he's sure very famous for them. Once again, their W/P aspect! That they are paradoxically both immediate and eternal - both instant, and continuous, which means there is no recognition time lag. They're in the mind already!*

The tremendous effectiveness of these unconscious projections is such that they not only give one the feeling of pointing to the ***ens realissimum*** (A term for God), but make one convinced that they actually express it (Godhead) and established it as a type of 'psychic' fact (Godzone).

It must be remembered that the image and its statement are psychic processes which are different from their transcendental object; they do not posit it, they merely point to it.

Many people are unable to separate the psychic fact from the unknowable metaphysical background. They directly equate the romantic image (e.g. the long haired Christ pic hanging on the wall) with the transcendental "Godzone" to which it points. This transference is unproblematic in the mind of the believer, and only comes unstuck when the believer attempts to communicate the absolute 'truth' of the experience.

It is impossible to prove God's reality to anyone outside of oneself, because faith in a mysterious divinity is not based on facts as such, but feelings. Feelings may be presumed, but cannot be communicated or proved outside of oneself.

> *JAN: I figure that Carl is here is starting to offer insights into his own personal Godzone...... when he states: "Psychic processes are different from their transcendental object; they do not posit it, they merely point to it", he is showing how he views the whole God situation - not so much a sentient being with all the attributes that facilitate cosmos making, but instead a continuously evolving expression of mankind's collective unconscious in seeking divine sanction.*
>
> *I'm not sure if he's said as much directly, but his writings continually allude to it....IMHO of course!*

In what follows I shall attempt a discussion of "coming to terms" with certain religious traditions and ideas.

> *JAN: In that last statement Carl shows he is not interested in issues surrounding Religious Dogma - the best or proper way to think/talk of God - such chat becomes a very much 'the bible says here/ the bible says there' double headbutt.*
>
> *Throughout the book CJ steers well clear, concentrating on the 'how's and why's' rather than dismissible facts - what he calls psychic facts as distinct from disputable physical facts......*

Since I shall be writing about the metaphysical realm, my ability to articulate my feelings is challenged quite as much as my thinking. I cannot, therefore, write objectively, but subjectively must introduce insights I have gained when reading certain books of the bible, or memories of my interrogations of the doctrines of our faiths.

I do not write as a biblical scholar (which I am not), but as a layman and physician who has been able to see deeply into the psychic life of many people. What I express is primarily my own personal view but I know that I also speak in the name of many who have had similar experiences.

By my response I hope to learn why, and to what purpose Job was wounded, and what consequences have resulted out of this for Yahweh as well as for man.

CARL G. JUNG

CHAPTER 6:
CARL JUNG'S
ANSWER TO JOB
rewritten by
John Andrew Nobbs

As far as I am concerned, the Book of Job is a landmark in the long historical development of mankind's search for and delineation of God. At the time the book was written, there were already many testimonies which had given a complex, darker picture of Yahweh – the portrait of both a generous and loving god, and one who also knew no moderation in his emotions and suffered profoundly from this lack of moderation. He himself admitted that he was eaten up with rage and jealousy and that this knowledge was painful to him. He was a God of opposites: insight existed along with obtuseness, loving kindness with cruelty, creative power with destructiveness. Everything was there, and none of these qualities seemed to be an obstacle to the other. Such a collision of emotional opposites within the same persona is only possible when very little or no reflecting consciousness (what might be called Wisdom) is present at all.

Whilst this lack of consciousness may seem at odds with his omniscience, the pattern of God's relationship with mankind bears this out. From the Garden of Eden on, the conscious/unconscious dichotomy is the central driver, and the flashpoint occurs when the side that is divine darkness is unveiled in the Book of Job.

Blake's Job Family before the catastrophes

> *JAN: Its worth observing that Satan's harassments started off subtly, with Job's first setbacks easily attributed, not to God, but to the depradations of various unkind 'other' tribes... hard to blame God for them.*
>
> *The second wave, where Job cops the bodily ailments, can more easily be pointed at the celestial one, especially since, after a while, Job could easily be thinking: "Hey! I'm not dead yet... What gives?"...*
>
> *But that raises the important question: Does Job know that God /Satan is responsible for his litany of catastrophes?*

As a response to Satan's obliterating nearly everything to do with his life, Job introduces himself to Yahweh thus:

"Behold, I am of small account; what shall I answer thee?

**I lay my hand on my mouth.
I Have spoken once, and I will not answer;**

Twice, but I'll proceed no further."

And indeed, in the immediate presence of the infinite power behind creation, this is the only possible answer for a witness is still trembling in every limb with the terror of imminent annihilation. What else could he reasonably answer in the circumstances?

In spite of his insignificant status, this man comprehends that he is confronted with a superhuman being who is hyper-sensitive and very easily provoked. Job also somehow knows that it is far better to withhold all mortal reflections, as well as saying nothing of any moral requirements which supposedly apply to a God.

Yahweh's "justice" is everywhere praised, so Job is hoping he could bring the complaint concerning his innocence before God as the just judge. But he doubt's this possibility:

"How can a man be just before God?"

Job wants to explain his point of view to Yahweh, to state his complaint, and tells him:

"Thou knowest that I am not guilty... I desire to argue my case with God. I know That I shall be vindicated."

WB's God looks iffy about things going on below

JAN: The line: **"I know That I shall be vindicated."** *is particularly telling, as J predicts his steadfastness, and time shows that he sticks to his guns-which makes him a particularly special human being, i.e. he has attributes of absolute conviction and truth that one might describe as Godlike. Later on, when CJ talks of Job 'outgooding' God, it started here when Job made his bold assertion..*

Job hopes that Yahweh will summon him and give him a reason, or at least allow him to plead his cause. Properly appreciating the disproportion between man and God, he asks:

"Wilt thou break a leaf driven to and fro? And will thou pursue the dry stubble?"

God has put him in the wrong, but there is no justice. He has:

"taken away my right."

"Till I die, I will not put away my integrity from me. I will hold fast to my righteousness, and will not let it go."

Job is never shaken in his faith, and has already uttered an important truth when he said:

"Behold, my witness is in heaven, and he that vouches for me is on high...."

"He would maintain the right of a man with God, like that of a man with his neighbour."

And later:

For I know that my vindicator lives, and al last he will stand upon the earth".

These words clearly show that Job, in spite of his doubt as to whether man can be justly treated before God, still finds it difficult to relinquish the idea of meeting God on the basis of justice and therefore of morality. Because, in spite of losing almost everything, he cannot give up his faith in divine justice.

Blake's 'And the devil went'... and, man, did he go!

It is not easy for Job to accept the knowledge that divine capriciousness breaks the law as whim takes it. On the other hand, he has to admit there's no-one except Yahweh himself that is doing him injustice. He cannot deny that he's up against a God who does not care a jot for any moral opinion and does not recognise any form of ethics as binding on himself (on others yes, but not him!).

This is perhaps the greatest thing about Job, that, faced with Yahweh's good/bad dichotomy, he still does not doubt the unity of God. As certain as he is of the bad in Yahweh, he is equally certain of the good. But, he clearly sees that God is at odds with himself – so at odds that ironically he, Job, is quite certain of finding in God a counsellor and an "advocate" against God.

Dont look up Dad! I alone was saved and came back apace.

> JAN: And it is spectacularly ironic, that God, through his cataclysmic interaction with Job, eventually resolves himself when he is incarnated as Jesus. Could that mean that God's long term intention (triggered by subliminal instinct rather than his rational side?) was to use Job's goodness to force him to face his dark side and to 'complete' his divided self.

God's creativity born of inner conflict

In a human being who renders us evil we cannot expect at the same time to find a supporter. But Yahweh is not a human being: He is both a persecutor and counsellor in one, and the one aspect is as real as the other. Yahweh is not split but is an antinomy- a totality of inner opposites– and this is the indispensable condition for his tremendous dynamism, omniscience and omnipotence.

The Celestial One Himself looking a bit uuurrr?

JAN: CJ has a tremendous insight here: The act of generation cannot occur without vigorous interaction between the creative aspect and its opposite-the destructive side. Jung posts that God's ability to make the universe is born out of a tremendous inner conflict. In the same way that human procreation is essentially viloent, God's creativity is enacted by the dynamic interaction between his good and bad side.

Later, its disappearance after the transition to the benign God as Christ, proves the point! After the birth of Jesus we hear no more of acts of creation. He has made the cosmos, he has made mankind, and he has remade himself as Christ.

The extreme self inflictive turbulence of the Job case results in Christ the 'meek', 'turn the other cheek', after which there is no need for God to countenance his dark side-it has been retired to the history of the Old Testament.

Why Does God fall for Satan's trap?

It is amazing to see how easily Yahweh, quite irrationally, had let himself be influenced by Satan's doubting thought, which made him unsure of Job's faithfulness.

Rather humanoid Satan applying the boils

JAN: Jung's first reference to Satan pitches him as an eternal 'evil' force co-existent with God's goodness, supplying the iniquitous balance to the just. Jung writes: ".... 'the evil one' existed before mankind as one of the 'Sons of God'".

Just above he also refers to Satan as a 'doubting thought'. As with the way he considers God, CJ has gone way past the caricature of Horned Devil. Instead Satan is viewed as both Son of God (and bad brother to Christ) as well as a projection of his persona (thought). This is another wave /particle paradox that cleverly resolves the metaphysical dichotomy......

This places Satan as an extension of God's DNA/ Unconscious dark side, and thus is capable of doing the dirty deeds, while God can pretend hands off! This is the reason Satan disappears (goes to the back of the brain) with the appearance of Christ as the 'all good' God.

With God's hair trigger suspiciousness the mere possibility of doubt was enough to infuriate him and induce that duplicity which he had shown in the Garden of Eden, when first he pointed out the Tree of Knowledge to Adam and Eve and at the same time forbad them to eat it, upon pain of death.

With this he precipitated the fall. Similarly, his faithful servant Job is now to be exposed to a violent moral test, quite gratuitously and to no purpose. Yahweh already knows Job is super faithful and constant and moreover He could have assured himself had He taken counsel with his own omniscience. Why, then, is the test made at all ?

From the human point of view Yahweh's behaviour is so obviously absurd that one has to ask oneself whether there is not an unspoken underlying motive driving it.

Had Yahweh some secret resistance or fear of Job? That would explain his yielding to Satan. But what might man possess that God does not have?

Because of his puniness when arrayed against the vast power of the Almighty, Job was unable to actively parry the onslaught. Instead he had to passively accept the situation and to exercise the rational side of his mind and develop 'wisdom'.

Wisdom is really another word for a more advanced consciousness based on deeper self reflection: Job, in order to survive, must always be 'mindful' of his impotence.

God had no need of this circumspection, for never previously had he come up against an insuperable obstacle that would force him to hesitate, and hence make him reflect on himself. This would have been unfamiliar territory for God.

A more conventional Blakean devil.

Did the fact that man might know something than God didn't arouse God's jealous suspicion. Suspicions of that kind might perhaps explain his behaviour ?. Too often before, human beings had not behaved in the proper manner. Even his trustworthy servant Job might have something up his sleeve. This would explain Yahweh's surprising readiness to listen to Satan's insinuations against his better judgement.

Why Job's torments and the divine wager should suddenly come to an end is not quite clear. So long as Job does not actually die, the pointless suffering could be continued indefinitely. We must, however, keep an eye on the possible backstory to this Job saga. It is just possible that some perceptions in God's psyche will gradually begin to take shape as a response to Job's undeserved suffering—something to which Yahweh, even if he had only a faint inkling of it, could hardly remain indifferent.

Suddenly, something has changed!
Without Yahweh's knowledge and contrary to his intentions, the tormented though guiltless Job has unexpectedly been lifted up to a superior knowledge of God, which even God himself did not possess. Had Yahweh consulted his omniscience, Job would not have had the advantage of him. But then, so many other things would not have happened either. There would be no necessity for God to atone, and there would be no need for the birth of Jesus Christ.

Job instinctively understands God's inner antimony, and innocently outlasts its chaotic intent. In the light of this besting, his knowledge attains a 'beyond' mortal numinosity resulting in man's god-likeness, which one would not expect from an ordinary human. Job, by his insistence on bringing his case before God, even without hope of a hearing, let alone a positive outcome, had stood his ground and thus created the very situation that forced God to reveal his true nature.

A tornado takes away the kids

> *JAN : Carl's interpretation here is profound and compelling. His vast experience trawling through examples of numinosity has equipped him with the ability to discern the psychic turning points in Job's saga.*
>
> *Jung's 'alchemical' awareness has revealed crucial interpretations un-procurable by your standard biblical scholar.*
>
> *And, once you bypass the standard supernatural religious dogma, and view the bible as a historical divine wishlist, the above interpretation makes a lot of*

God does not apologise

With this dramatic climax Yahweh abruptly breaks off his cruel game of cat and mouse. But no-one should expect that his wrath will now be turned against Satan the slanderer. Yahweh does not think of bringing this mischief making son of his to account, nor does it ever occur to him to give Job at least the moral satisfaction of explaining his behaviour.

Instead he comes riding along on the tempest of his almightiness and thunders approaches at the half crushed human worm:

"Who is this that darkens counsel by words without insight?"

In view of the subsequent words of Yahweh, one must really ask oneself who is darkening what counsel? The only dark thing here is how Yahweh ever came to make a bet with Satan. It is certainly not Job who has darkened anything, and least of all a counsel. The bet does not contain any 'counsel' so far as one can see – unless of course, it was Yahweh himself who egged Satan on for the ultimate purpose of exalting Job.

And the Lord answered Job out of the whirlwind, looking a bit calm if you ask me

> *JAN: With that last line, has CJ landed on the deep purpose of the Job Saga???? Increasingly as one ponders the spiritual anomaly of "Why do bad things happen to good people", it becomes more possible to see the Book of Job as part of God's instinctive long term intentions.*
>
> *Did God use Job, Satan, and the whole cast as a strategy for his own conscious completion that peaked with the birth and death of Christ? A big call maybe, but makes as much, if not more sense than any other explanation....*

What insight is God talking about ?

Whose words without insight is God talking about? Presumably Yahweh is not referring to the words of Job's friends, but is rebuking Job. But what is Job's guilt? The only thing he can be blamed for is his incurable optimism in believing that he can appeal to divine justice. In this he is mistaken, as Yahweh's subsequent words prove.

God does not want to be just; he merely flaunts might over right. Job could not get that into his head, because he looked upon God as a moral being. He had never doubted God's might, but had hoped for right as well. But as he began to recognise God's contradictory nature, he assigned a limit to God's justice and goodness. So one can hardly speak of lack of insight.

With dreams upon my bed thou affrightest me.. Too Right!

> *JAN: Another way to put it is to ask if Job knows more than he lets on. By 'assigning a limit to God's justice', has Job worked out a way to deal with God? And if he's got this far, how much more does he understand about God that he not only doesn't divulge, but which knowledge doesn't change his response?*

Yahweh's Conundrum

The only answer to Yahweh's conundrum is therefore that it is Yahweh himself who darkens his own counsel and who has no insight. He tries to spin it back on Job and blames him for what he himself does. Man is not permitted to have an opinion about God, and, in particular, is to have no insight which God himself does not possess.

For seventy one verses he vituperatively proclaims his cosmos-creating power to his miserable victim, who sits in a pile of sh-t scratching his sores. Job has absolutely no need of being impressed by further exhibitions of this power. Yahweh, in his omniscience, should have known just how incongruous his attempts at intimidation were in such a situation. He could easily have seen that Job believes in God's omnipotence as much as ever and has never doubted it or wavered in his loyalty.

Yahweh pays so little attention to Job's dutiful and passive response that one suspects him of having an ulterior motive which is more important because it arouses fear in him. Only in the face of something frightening does one let off a cannonade of references to one's power, cleverness, courage, invincibility, etc.

And the spirit passed

> *JAN: Tremendous insight here, where Jung has revealed God's considerable fear. God's thunderings are text book rantings by someone in denial about the primal shock they have suffered from a sudden revelation. As Jung points out, God's 71 verse list of achievements, flung at Job as if he's a dart board, are in fact the private emotional* **cri de coeur** *of a selfbruised ego. It's a cry of hatred directed at himself. Perhaps that part of himself that is Satan, who as has been noticed, is co-eternal with God, which is another way of saying he is God's left hand.*

I consider that God's thunderings at Job so completely missed the point that one cannot help but see how much he is self absorbed.

This tremendous emphasis he outlays on his omnipotence and greatness only makes sense when aimed at a listener who doubts it. The only 'doubter' is Satan, who has deceived him. So God's railing is very much against his own dark side for seducing his good side.

Yahweh must have seen Job's loyalty was unshakeable and that Satan had lost his bet. He must also have realised that, in accepting this bet, he had done everything possible to drive his faithful servant to disloyalty, even to the extent of perpetrating a series of heinous crimes. Yet it is not remorse and certainly not a moral horror that rises as consciousness, but a denied sense of emptiness that questions his omnipotence.

He is particularly sensitive on this point, because 'might' is the great argument. But omniscience knows that 'might' excuses nothing. The explosion walks back to the extremely uncomfortable fact that Yahweh had let himself be bamboozled by Satan. This weakness of his does not reach full consciousness, because Satan is treated with remarkable tolerance, so much so that Satan's intrigue is deliberately overlooked at Job's expense.

Luckily enough, Job had noticed during this harangue that everything else had been mentioned except his right to be heard. He has understood that it is at present impossible to argue the question of his right.

When the morning stars sang together and the sons of God shouted with joy.... Job's looking forward to this, but it's not on the horizon yet!

As well, whether Job realises what violence Yahweh is doing to his own omniscience by behaving like this we do not know, but his silence and submission leave a number of possibilities open. Job has no alternative but to formally revoke his demand for justice, and he therefore answers in the words quoted at the beginning:

"I lay my hand on my mouth."

He betrays not the slightest trace of mental reservation–in fact, his answer leaves us in no doubt that he has succumbed completely and without question to the tremendous force of the divine demonstration.

I am young and thee are very old. Hmmmm?

JAN: Has Job been smart enough to perceive that God's harangue is all bark and no bite? And is he even smarter to hide this knowledge from God, by tugging the forelock and lying doggo. Quite possibly Job figured that although smitten with boils, etc:

"Things might be looking bad, but I'm not dead yet!"

Maybe he's worked out he's not going to be killed and if he knows he won't be killed, isn't it just a game? And if he sticks to the rules, he could play for a draw....

I imagine the most exacting tyrant should have been satisfied with this, could be quite sure that his servant—from terror alone, to say nothing of never say die loyalty—would not dare to nourish a single improper thought for a very long time to come.

Strangely enough, Yahweh does not notice anything of the kind. He does not consider Job and his situation at all. It is rather as if he had another powerful opponent in the place of Job, one was better worth challenging.

This is clear from this twice repeated taunt:

"Gird up your loins like a man; I will question you."

I would have to choose positively grotesque examples to match the disproportion between two antagonists. But obviously Yahweh doesn't see it that way. He sees something in Job which is not normally found in man, but only in a God. Which is an equivalent moral strength which causes him to bring out his whole power apparatus and parade it before his opponent. Yahweh projects on to Job a sceptic's face which is hateful to him because it is his own, and which gazes at him with an unintentional but critical eye.

Spooked, Yahweh cannot rest satisfied with the first victorious around. Job has long since been overwhelmed, but the Almighty, whose 'doubting thought' Satan is transferred to the pitiable sufferer, still stands empty handed, faced by the phantom antagonist of his own shadow.

Therefore Yahweh raises his arm again:

**"Will you even put me in the wrong?
Will you condemn me that you may be justified?**

Have you an arm like God,
and can you thunder with a voice like his?"

Blake Red Dragon, but might as well be Satan and a great name: " The Number of the beast is 666"

Man, without protection and stripped of his rights, and whose nothingness is thrown in his face at every opportunity, evidently appears to be so dangerous to Yahweh he must be battered down with the heaviest artillery.

What irritates Yahweh can be seen from his challenge to Job:

"Look on every one that is proud, and bring him low; And tread down the wicked where they stand. Hide them in the dust together; bind their faces in the hidden place. Then will I also acknowledge to you that your own right hand can give you victory"

Job is challenged as though he himself were a demi God. But there is no other demi god except Satan, who owns Yahweh's ear. He is the only one who can pull the wool over God's eyes and put him up to a massive violation of his own moral code. A formidable opponent indeed, and, because of his close kinship, so close that he must be concealed with denial-even to the point of God's hiding him from his own consciousness!

I adjudge that in his stead God must set up his miserable servant as the torturee whom he has to fight, in the hope that by banishing the dreaded 'doubting thought' to the 'hidden place' he will be able to maintain himself in a state of unconsciousness.

JAN: Another crashing insight from Carl! The denial of Satan's role, i.e. the denial of the functioning of his own dark side is deeper proof of God's desire to remain in an unconscious state. And, the 'overclocked' tantrums are the audio visual portrait of the ego being dragged kicking and screaming to accepting a thorough transformation...

This further bolsters Jung's central Jobian premise-God's gaining of consciousness through incarnating as Jesus Christ...

Job being implored by those who do not get it

The unconscious self-inflicted trauma caused by the overheated self justification becomes even more acute for Yahweh due to unexpected consequences.

I think that the new consequence is something that has never occurred before in the history of the world, the fact that, without knowing it or wanting it, mortal man is raised by his moral behaviour to the level of the Gods, from which position he can apprehend the back of Yahweh, the abysmal world of 'shards'.

> *JAN: CJ does it again! He has figured out that Job got the chance to open the last door and see into the last room in God's psyche. For the first time man knows the full extent of God, and not by his personal design or ambition, but by God's own actions.*
>
> *The next question becomes: "If God is Omniscient, did he do this deliberately, or was he instinctively driven by his Unconscious?"*

Job contemplating wisdom while being ambidextrous

Does Job know what he has seen? If he does, he is astute or canny enough not to betray it. But his words speak volumes:

**"I know that thou canst do all things,
And that no purpose of thine can be thwarted."**

Truly, Yahweh can do all things and permits himself anything without batting an eyelid. With brazen countenounce he can unleash his shadow side and still remain unconscious at man's expense. He can boast of this superior power and enact laws which mean less than air to him. Rape and murder are mere bagatelles, and if he changes his mood he can play the feudal seigneur and generously recompense his bond-slave for the havoc wrought in his life:

**"So you have lost your sons and daughters?
No harm done, I'll give you new and better ones."**

Job continues (*no doubt with downcast eyes and in a low voice*):

"Therefore I have uttered which I did not understand, things too wonderful for me, which I did not know."

"I had heard of thee by the hearing of the ear, But now my eyes see thee…"

Guileless as Job's speech sounds, I think it could just as well be equivocal. He has learnt his lesson well and experienced 'wonderful things' which are none too easily grasped. Before, he had known Yahweh by the 'hearing of the ear', but now he has got a taste of his reality – an insightful lesson. Shrewdly, Job retreats from Yahweh's aggressive words and prostrates himself at his feet as if he were indeed the defeated.

But now my eyes see thee, and all the way to the back door

JAN: A surprising twist when Job declares that while he used to hear about God (Job makes it sound like hearsay chit chat), now he can see him. Sight is a far more concrete affirmation than sound! Analogous to finally meeting someone having heard about them for a while. A series of rumours becomes a fact! Job obviously senses that his knowledge of God has achieved another level.

While he's clever enough to bow down (the first time he has done so) and not let the new status go to his head, its such statements as this that may have hit home with God, making the almighty realise that mankind had caught up. In order to stay ahead of the gentry, he'd better come up with a new shift-self renewal, maybe!

Formerly he was naive, dreaming perhaps of a 'totally good' God, a benevolent ruler and just judge. He had imagined that a 'covenant' was a binding legal matter and that anyone who was party to a contract could insist on the terms as agreed; that God would be faithful and true, and, as one could assume from the 10 commandments, that God would have some recognition of ethical values or at least feel committed to his own legal standpoint.

But, to his horror, he has discovered that Yahweh is not human but, in certain respects, lesser then human; that he is just what Yahweh himself says of Leviathon (the crocodile):

"He beholds everything that is high: He is king over all proud beasts."

Unconsciousness has an animal nature. Like all old gods Yahweh has his animal symbolism with its unmistakable borrowings from the much older very **theriomorphic** (having animal form) gods of Egypt. This animalistic tendency explains Yahweh's behaviour, which, from the human point of view, is so impossible: It is the behaviour of an unconscious being who cannot be judged morally. Yahweh is a phenomenon, as Job says, "not a man".

Behemoth, to tell the truth looking rather cuddly, showing that Blake was essentially a kindly soul

> *JAN: CJ goes into this animal/unconscious analogy often in other writings. In **Answer to Job** he mentions it only once. Nevertheless the animal/uncon match is a cornerstone of his thinking.*
>
> *Witness the names **animus** and **anima**, which articulate the unspoken energies inhabiting the opposite sex. Animus is the male principle residing in a woman's mind, and vice versa.*
>
> *Jung's identifying of same demonstrates his deep pursuit of the stimulae in human nature, which enabled the compelling commentary of Job.*

Omniscience on the horizon.

Yahweh eventually calmed down. I imagine the therapeutic stance of unresisting acceptance had proved its value. Nevertheless, Yahweh is still somewhat critical of Job's friends: they 'have not spoken of me what is right'.

The projection of his doubt complex extends, comically enough, to these respectable and slightly pedantic old gents, as though it mattered what they thought.

One can hardly avoid the impression that God's Omniscience is gradually drawing near to a revelation, accompanied by fears of self-destruction engendered by the sort of doubt that comes with self discovery.

Fortunately, Job's final surrender is so complete that one could assume with some certainty that, for all the protagonists, the incident is closed for good and all.

However we, the commenting chorus on this great drama, do not feel quite like that. For our moral sensibilities, it is by no means apparent that with Job's profound obeisance and prudent silence, a real answer has been given to the question raised by the Satanic wager with God.

Job has not so much answered as retreated in a politically adept way. In so doing he displayed remarkable self-discipline, but an unequivocal answer has still to be given.

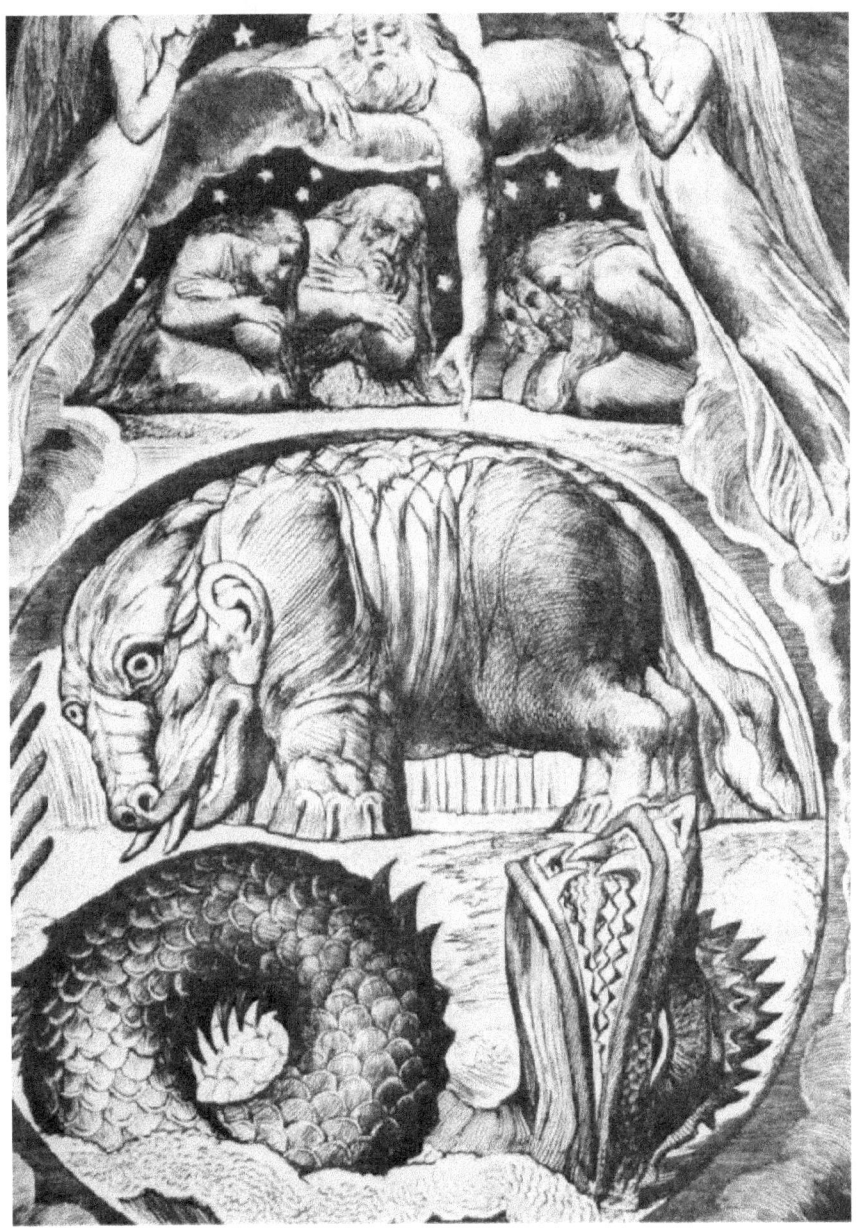

The full pic. God telling the gang: "You have no idea of what I am capable!"… actually the people have a pretty good idea, already!

To take the most obvious point, what about the moral wrong Job has suffered? How does that sit with the fact that mankind is needed by Yahweh and that it obviously matters to God whether men speak 'right' of him or not.

He needs Job's loyalty, and it means so much to him that he shrinks at nothing in carrying out his test. This attitude attaches an almost divine title on man, for what else is there that could mean anything to a God who has everything?

It is obvious to me that Yahweh's divided attitude, which on the one hand tramples on human life and happiness without regard, and on the other hand must have man for a partner, puts both in a problematic position.

At any one moment Yahweh behaves as irrationally as a cataclysm; the next moment he wants to be loved, honoured, worshipped, and praised as just. He reacts irritably to every word that has the faintest suggestion of criticism, while he himself does not give a damn for his own moral standing if his actions run counter to his rules.

One can submit only to such a capricious God with fear, trembling, unctuous praises and ostentatious obedience. But a relationship of trust seems completely out of the question to our modern way of thinking. Moral satisfaction cannot be expected from an unconscious god of this kind.

Nevertheless Job got his satisfaction, without Yahweh's intending it and possibly without even knowing it, as the writer would have it appear. Yahweh's allocutions have the unintended, yet none the less transparent, purpose of showing Job his brutal power:

"This is I, the creator of all the ungovernable, ruthless forces of nature, which are not subject to any ethical laws. I too am an amoral force of nature, a purely phenomenal personality that cannot see its own back."

Job doing the right thing

> JAN: Interesting that God should be describing nature as though he's referring to unconscious forces, the same sort of unconscious forces that swirl inside his own mind.
>
> When he refers to: "forces of nature, which are not subject to any ethical laws", he is talking about his own conduct, not just his creations. God himself is validating Jung's judgement of him.... it's in the scriptures!

I think this is a moral satisfaction of the first order for mankind, because, through witnessing this declaration mankind, in spite of his impotence, has become an arbiter over God. I do not know whether Job really realises this, but we do know from numerous commentaries on Job that all succeeding ages have overlooked the fact that a kind of fate affects Yahweh, causing him to give himself away so blatantly - he has unwittingly raised Job to equality by humiliating him.

The divine shift has been consummated for all eternity. Yahweh's dual nature has been revealed, and man directly, and God indirectly, have registered this fact. Such a revelation, whether man understood or not, could not fail to have far-reaching consequences.

The Appearance of Sophia

Before proceeding with the purgation of the divine drama, I must turn back to the time that the Book of Job was written. Although the dating is uncertain, it is generally assumed tht it was written between 600 and 300 BC. Not too long before the book of Proverbs (400 to 300 BC).

In Proverbs we encounter the injection of Greek cosmology, the influence that informs the rest of the story. This is the idea of Sophia (Greek for wisdom). For the purposes of the next stage Sophia is **Sapienta Dei** (the wisdom of God), who is co-eternal with him and a more or less concrete manifestation of Feminine nature.

I'm intrigued by Sophia's appearance as emblematic of Yahweh's evolving metaphysical 'marriage' with mankind. From the ancient records we know that the divine drama was initiated between God and his people, who were then betrothed to him, as a female principle being conjoined with God's masculine dynamis, and over whose faithfulness he watched jealously.

Blake's benevolent feminine wisdom caring for the world

A particular example of this jealousy is the trials of Job, whose faith is subjected to a savage test. As I have said before, the really astonishing thing is how easily Yahweh gives in to the insinuations of Satan. If it were true that he trusted Job perfectly, it would be only logical for Yahweh to defend him, unmask the malicious slanderer and make him pay for his defamation of God's faithful servant.

But Yahweh never thinks of this, not even after Job's innocence has been proved. We hear nothing of a rebuke of Satan. Therefore we cannot doubt Yahweh's connivance (JN: *Satan as part of God's psyche?*).

His readiness to deliver Job into Satan's malign hands proves that he doubts Job precisely because he projects his own tendency to unfaithfulness on to an innocent scapegoat.

I think there is reason to suspect that God is about to loosen his matrimonial ties with Israel (*JAN: Divorce of the Jews to switch to a 'marriage' with Christians?*) but hides his intention from himself. This vaguely suspected unfaithfulness causes him, with the help of Satan, to seek out the unfaithful one.

He infallibly picks on the most faithful of the lot, who is forthwith subjected to a gruelling test. Yahweh has become unsure of his own faithfulness.

At about the same time, I feel he senses he has to re-introduce a feminine influence from the beginning of the world, a type of psychic consort whose name is **Sophia**.

Why doesn't Carl refer to Sophia as God's Anima? Seems a good match, especially since he invented the concept.....

God's getting of Wisdom

There is a necessity for the appearance of Sophia, whose feminine care and compassion would be a leavening balance to God's harsh male power. Things simply could not go on as before. The supposed 'just' God could not go on committing injustices, and the 'omniscient' could not behave any longer like an erratic human being.

If Job gains knowledge of God, then God must also learn to know himself. It just could not be that Yahweh's dual nature should become public knowledge and remain hidden from himself alone. Whoever knows God has an effect on him. The failure of the attempt to corrupt Job has changed Yahweh's nature. Self reflection becomes a necessity, and for this wisdom is needed.

Because man feels himself at the mercy of Yahweh's capricious will, he is in need of wisdom. Not so Yahweh, who up to the Job fracas has had nothing to contend with except man's insignificant transgressions.

With the Job drama, I believe the situation undergoes a radical change. Suddenly Yahweh comes up against a man who stands firm, who clings to his rights even though he is compelled to surrender to brute force.

Because of this a human by the name of Job has seen through to the back of God and the unconscious split in his nature for the first time. God was now known, and this knowledge went on working not only in Yahweh but in mankind as well.

This is actually Job with his daughters, where are the boys?

> *JAN: A bit of a leap of faith here from CJ... Sophia sprung out of the thin air like that! But it does talk to the evolution of the Christian God, with feminine aspects, as a departure from the hard Judaic God.*
>
> *Assuming that Sophia exists as an influence in the birth of Jesus, Jung also astutely prefigures that the spiritual importance of Mary would amplify throughout the common era. The culture of Mary within the church only reached its apogee around the 12 Century AD.*
>
> *So the introduction of Sophia pre Christ, makes a lot of sense given the long term evolution of the softer Christian God...*

Thus it was that Yahweh reconnected with the gentle touch of the eternal Sophia, whose feminine essence would compliment Yahweh and his attitude, and at the same time reaffirm his Wisdom.

The same Wisdom, in the form of Sophia, that acts for men as a compassionate advocate against the brutal side of Yahweh, and shows them the bright golden side, the kind, just, and amiable aspect of God.

The reappearance of Sophia points to a coming act of procreation. Her eternal coexistence with Yahweh signifies the perpetual **Heiros Gamos** (*sacred marriage between male and female divinities*) in which worlds are begotten and born. A momentous change is imminent: God desires to regenerate himself using the mystery of the cosmic nuptials, and to become man.

The appointment of Mary: The second 'Eve'

The approach of Sophia betokens a new creation. But this time it is not the world that is to be changed; rather it is God who intends to change his own nature.

Mankind is not, as before, to be destroyed, but this time saved. In this decision we can discern the 'philanthropic' influence of Sophia: no new human beings are actually created, but only a half God-half man.

For this purpose a new and unique procedure must be employed. The second Adam shall not, like the first, proceed directly from the hand of the creator, but shall be born of a human.

A pretty intense WB pic of a women who could be a be cracked concrete 20th C Mary

So this time priority falls to the 'Second Eve', not only in a spiritual sense but in a material sense as well. Thus Mary, the virgin, is chosen as the pure vessel for the coming birth of God. Her independence of the male is emphasised by her virginity as the essential condition of the process.

She is a 'daughter of God' who, as the later writings confirm, is distinguished from the outset by the privilege of Immaculate Conception and thus free from the taint of original sin. Freedom from original sin marks her out as belonging to the state of purity before the fall.

I imagine this posits a new beginning. The divine immaculateness of her status makes it immediately clear that she not only bares the image of God in complete purity, but, as the bride of God, is also the incarnation of her prototype namely Sophia.

Her love of mankind, widely emphasised in the ancient writings, suggests that in this newest creation, Yahweh has allowed himself to be profoundly affected by Sophia.

For Mary, the blessed among women, is a friend and intercessor for all sinners. Like Sophia, she's a mediatrix who leads the way to God and assures God's forgiveness of mankind.

God waking up to himself

> JAN: Mary has, especially since the second millennium, become the overt face of compassion within the Christian faith.
>
> Carl doesn't quite say so, but if you watch the overall trajectory of the Virgin Mary in the rule book, it is quite plain that that role has been unconsciously verified by the vast throng of ordinary people who find the maternal instinct undismissable.
>
> A mother's unlimited love for her progeny has been transposed to the Godzone....

As the pride of God and Queen of Heaven Mary continues the importance of the old Testament Sophia.

Remarkable indeed are the unusual precautions that confirm the importance of Mary: immaculate conception, extirpation of the taint of original sin, everlasting virginity. I think the Mother of God is obviously being protected against Satan's tricks.

From this we can conclude that Yahweh has consulted his own omniscience. In his omniscience there is a clear awareness of the perverse capability which lurks in the dark son of God.

Mary must at all costs be protected from these corrupting influences. The inevitable consequence of all these elaborate measures is something that has not been sufficiently recognised in the theological commentary of the Incarnation: her freedom from original sin sets Mary apart from mankind in general, whose common characteristic is original sin and therefore in need of redemption.

By having these special attributes applied to her, Mary is elevated to the status of a goddess and consequently loses something of her humanity: she will not conceive her son in sin like all other mothers, and also, he will never be a true human being, but a God.

To my knowledge no one has ever perceived that this queers the pitch for a complete Incarnation of God, or rather, that incarnation is only partially consummated. Both mother and son are not real human beings at all, but half gods.

A Willy Boschian sort of a pic...but friendlier

> JAN: Carlo has got an interesting take there, and it is but one of the many insights of his that make his **Answer to Job** so inspirational.

Why incarnation?

All the universe is God's, and God is in all the universe from the very beginning. Why then the tour de force of the Incarnation? God is supposedly in everything already, so there must be something missing if a sort of second phase of creation is now required.

Since creation is universal, reaching to the remotest stellar galaxies on a macro level, and on a micro level it has also made organic life capable of endless differentiation, we cannot see where the defect lies.

I think that the argument that says that Christ had to appear in order to deliver mankind from evil is simplistic.

When one considers that evil was originally slipped into the scheme of things by Satan, and to which he continues to add, then it would seem much simpler if Yahweh would, once and for all, call this 'practical joker' severely to account, get rid of his pernicious influence, and thus eliminate the root of all evil.

He would then not need the elaborate arrangement of a special incarnation with all the unforeseeable consequences which it entails.

God's left hand?

> *JAN: But then that would be excising a part of his own mind...Hmmmmm.... Dark and malign it may be, it is still part of his psyche, and like matter, cannot be destroyed?*

What does it mean when God becomes man? It means nothing less than a universe shaking transformation of God. It means more or less what creation meant in the beginning, namely a second and final objectification of God.

At the time of the creation he revealed himself in nature; now he wants to be more specific and become man. It must be admitted, however, that there had been pointers in this direction before.

For, even though there were other human beings, (*JN: e.g. Neanderthals, Homo Erectus, were drowned in the Noah flood- interesting notion, but a bit discriminatory*) who had evidently been created before Adam, Yahweh decided to create, by a special act of generation, a new human who was the image of God.

I judge that the creation of Adam in his own image was the first step in God becoming man. He admitted Adam's descendants, especially the tribe of Israel, into his personal cosmology, and progressively instructed his 'chosen' people through the infusion of their prophets with his spirit.

All these things were preparatory events and symptoms of a urgency within God to become man.

Invention of Monotheism

JAN: This is not really a CJ thing, but if inverted adds up the same way: The Jews were the first nation to conceive of a monotheistic God i.e. A God who was everywhere/all the time. Prior to that all gods were of a certain space and/or time e.g. Anuket was the Egyptian goddess of the Nile, so when around the Nile you had to do the right things by Her, but unnecessary when not nearby . This meant she had special rites and rules, not applicable to other gods... when you add all the gods of time and space together, you get a forest of rules and regs, most of which would be counter indicative... very confusing, but when you have a God that's everywhere and who never sleeps: one set of rules for everybody! Very clever!

As well, Gods of time and space can be destroyed/superceded,e.g. when the Babylonians got clobbered by Cyrus the Great, bang went Baal... Cyrus also said to the captive Jews:"Go back to Israel and reset your relationship with Yahweh"! Which you can do with a God that transcends time and space...

On top of this the Jews went one step further: They said that God made man in his own image (of course one could also invert it, CJ like: The Jews invented a God in their own image !!!!) That is to say that they are the race of God....hence the chosen ones....

That anthropomorphism posits that the Jewish God has become an ideation of Man, and vice versa. As the image of God and man become increasingly conjoined in a plastic metaphysical sense, any breakdowns are temporary and re-negotiatable..

Christianity took this 'race of God' a step further: Mankind became part of God's family! Because there is no such closer tie than spiritual blood, Christianity is the final instalment in God zone ideation...

But from very early on, throughout the world there had existed a proclivity for the duality; the human nature of God to be married with the divine nature of man. That is why, long before Genesis was written, we find corresponding tendencies in ancient Egyptian records.

These intimations of pre-figuration's of the Incarnation point to a shift in the evolution of mankind's spiritual agenda. But Pre-figurations, however are not in themselves creative events; they are only pointers to the coming conscious activation.

What, then, is the real reason for the incarnation as an historical event?

In order to answer this question I have to go rather far back. As we have seen, Yahweh evidently has a disinclination to use his omniscience as a reflective balance to his omnipotence.

The most instructive example of this is his relationship to Satan: it always looks as if Yahweh was unaware of his dark son's malign interventions. This is because God never seems to consult his own absolute knowledge.

I can only make sense of this by assuming that Yahweh was so fascinated by his successful act of creation, that he forgot about his omniscience altogether. It is quite understandable that the magical bodying forth of the most diverse objects, which had never before existed in such pristine splendour, should have caused God infinite delight.

The book of Job still rings with the proud joy of creating when Yahweh points to the huge animals he has successfully turned out:

"Behold Behemoth, which I made as I made you."

Worth another look because this is what the ratrod will approximate, but more of an Aussie wombat version

> JAN: Both Behemoth and Leviathon are mentioned in passing in the book of Job, and both are big dark things, especially WB's Leviathon. So, stacked against Job's puniness, God seems pretty keen to show Job the deep, dark side of his creativity.

So, even in Job's time, I consider that Yahweh is still intoxicated with the tremendous power and grandeur of his creation. Compared with this, what are Satan's pinpricks and the lamentations of human beings? Yahweh must have been blinded by his self satisfaction, otherwise he would never have ridden so roughshod over Job's human dignity.

Satan knew how to make more frequent and better use of omniscience than his father. It was he who placed the unforeseen challenge of Job's goodness in Yahweh's way, which God's omniscience knew to be indispensable for the completion of the divine drama. For God's psychic completion the case of Job was decisive, and it could only have happened because of Satan's provocation.

Of course, in God's overarching omniscience, consciousness has existed for all eternity, and it is probable that the unacknowledged presence of it instinctively pressured him into fabricating the brutal testing of Job in order that he would force himself to become conscious, and thus gain new insights into himself.

The inverted victory of the oppressed Job is definitive: Job stands morally higher than Yahweh. In this respect the creature has cataclysmically surpassed the creator. When such an external stimulus impacts on an unconscious inner knowledge, this knowledge can stimulate consciousness. Something of the kind must have happened to Yahweh. Job's moral superiority cannot be refuted.

Although he did not immediately become conscious of the moral defeat he had suffered at Job's hands, a change gradually comes over Yahweh's behaviour after the Job episode.

This points to God's recognition of the metaphysical forces which are preparing to manifest in his consciousness. In all this, as we have said, we discern the reintroduction of Sophia.

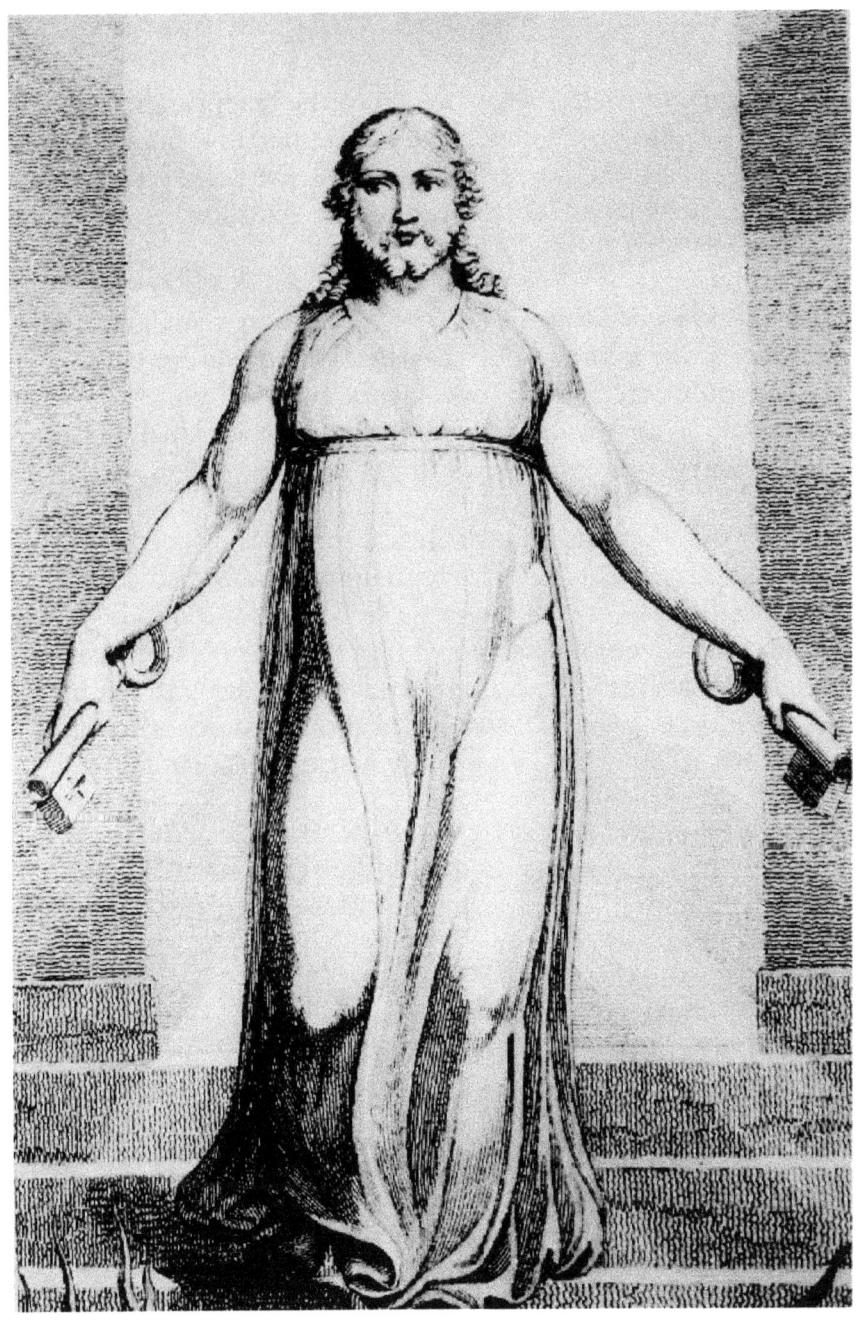

Christ with the keys to…..???

Considering Yahweh's behaviour up to the reappearance of Sophie as a whole, one factor is always apparent – his actions are all characterised by a lack of consciousness. Time and again there is an absence of reflection and disregard for his own self knowledge.

His consciousness seems to be not much more than a primitive 'alertness', which knows no self-reflection and no morality. Yahweh only perceives and acts instinctively, without consideration of any of his subjects, whose individual powerlessness presents no threat.

Hence a situation arises in which real reflection is needed. That is why Sophia is required. Her femininity stimulates the much needed reflection, which triggers Yahweh's decision to become a man. It is a decision charged with profound consequences: he initiates consciousness by indirectly acknowledging that Job (*JAN: Acting on behalf of mankind?*) is morally superior to him and he has to atone in the only way he can - become human!

I sense that he has already invented the world, he has already invented man. The only way to re-stabilise his cosmos is for him to reinvent himself, to rebirth himself as one of the subjects he has created - a human being.

Had he not taken this decision he would have found himself in flagrant opposition to his omniscience. Yahweh must become man precisely because he has done man a wrong.

God, the guardian of justice, knows that every wrong must be expiated, and wisdom knows that His moral law is above even him. Because his creature has surpassed him he must regenerate himself.

God thinks! Hmmmmmm..

To sum up: the stimulus for the incarnation lies in Job's elevation and its ulterior purpose is the fostering of the completion of Yahweh's consciousness. For this to happen, a momentous change was needed, a pivot charged with effect, without which no higher level of consciousness can be reached.

I now wish to convey how the impending birth of the Son of God fits with the general pattern of the hero's life which has been established for millennia and handed down by tradition.

Since this son is not intended merely as a national Messiah, but as the universal saviour of mankind, we have also to consider the pagan myths and revelations surrounding the life of one who is singled out by the gods.

The birth of Christ is therefore characterised by the established precepts attendant on the birth of the hero, such as the annunciation, divine generation from a virgin, the recognition of the birth of a king, the persecution of the newborn, his flight and concealment, his lowly birth, etc.

In addition, the motif of the emergence of the hero is discernible in the wisdom of the 12 year old child in the temple, and there are several examples in the gospels of the breaking away from the mother.

A quite special interest attaches to the character and fate of the incarnate son of God. Seen from a distance of 2000 years, it is impossible to reconstruct a biographical picture of Christ from the writings that have been preserved.

No eyewitness texts exist. The historically verifiable facts are scanty, and the little biographically vaild material that exists is insufficient to map out a consistent career or even a remotely probable character.

Actually this is Urizen, but characteristic enough to be Job

Certain theologians have discovered the main reason for this is the fact that Christ's life and psychology cannot be separated from eschatology.

Eschatology means in effect that Christ is God and man at the same time and that he therefore suffers a Divine as well as a human fate. The two natures interpenetrate so far that any attempt to separate them mutilates both.

The Divine overshadows the human. Jesus Christ is scarcely graspable as a real personality. Every attempt to single out one particular feature does disservice to the other, either with respect to his divinity or with respect to his humanity. The commonplace is so interwoven with the miraculous and the mythical that we can never be sure of the facts.

Perhaps the most disturbing and confusing thing of all is that the oldest writings, those of St Paul, do not seem to have the slightest interest in Christ's existence as a real human being. The synoptic gospels are equally unsatisfactory as they have more the character of propaganda than of biography.

With regard to the human side of Christ, if I can speak about a 'purely human' aspect at all, what stands out most clearly is his love of mankind. This feature is already prefigured in the relationship with Mary to Sophia, and especially in his procreation by the Holy Ghost, whose feminine nature is exemplified and manifested by Sophia.

There is no evidence that Christ ever wondered about himself, or that he ever confronted himself.

Christ possibly talking to himself in the wilderness

> *JAN: Hey, Carl! You're wrong on this one... how about the forty days in the wilderness? I think they'd be a fair amount of soul searching and self interrogation going on there...*

To this rule there's only one significant exception – the despairing cry from the cross:

"My God! My God! Why has thou forsaken me?"

I think this to be a very concrete example of human nature attaining divinity; at that moment God (as Christ) experiences what it means to be mortal, and drinks to the dregs what he made his faithful servant Job suffer. Here is given the answer to Job and clearly this supreme moment is as divine as it is human, as 'eschatological' as it is 'psychological'.

At the moment of the cry from the cross, not only can one feel the human so absolutely, the divine myth is also present in full force. Both mean one and the same thing.

How then, can one possibly 'demythologise' the figure of Christ? A rationalistic attempt of that sort would suck out all of his mystery, and what remained would no longer be the birth and tragic fate of a God in time.

Instead, he'd be treated as a barely authenticated religious teacher, a Jewish reformer who was Hellenistically interpreted and misunderstood – a prophet like Buddha or Mohammed, but certainly not a manifestation of God incarnate.

Jesus talking to God's left hand

*JAN: CJ's understanding here is right on the money! And he can accept the paradox because he is adjudging in a wave/particle duality (**WPD**). WPD means rather than looking at one to the exclusion of the other, you 'look' between the two, 'feeling' both at the same time.*

This is moving away from a critical facts and figures Modus Operandi, which is very appropriate for building aeroplanes, but not much help when pondering the mysteries of life and death.

This attitude has enabled Jung to present the case for the divine /human paradigm that satisfies a devout Post Christian, for whom the dogmatic interpretation of the bible is a bridge too far.

The Myth of Christ

What would be the consequences of a Christ disinfected of all trace of eschatology? Today we have a rationalistic psychology, which attempts to scientifically define Christ's messages as if they were specimens under a microscope. When you regard them from such a 'rational' point of view, such statements are detached from their mythical context, and are easily dismissed as personal idiosyncracy.

But what sort of conclusion are we bound to arrive at if a statement like:

"I am the Way, the truth and the life; no one comes to the Father, but by me"….

….. is reduced to personal psychology? Obviously the same conclusion as that reached by Jesus' relatives when, in their ignorance of Christ's godly provenance, they said:

"He is beside himself."

What is the use of a religion without a mythos, since religion means, at the end of the day, a mechanism which grounds us by linking back to the eternal myth?

God striking Adam: the way of the old Testa

> *JAN: Carlo is demonstrating the dilemma facing humanity in an age of 'reason'- if you try to take the mystery out of religious beliefs, there's not much left and it has no power.*
>
> *Religion's purpose is to soften the Sturm und Drang of mortality, by posting a formal etiquette around its trajectory. So, like its purpose, it is not scientifically explicable.*

I know that it has often been assumed, perhaps as the result of a dissatisfaction with the obscure factual material, that Christ was nothing but a myth; no more than a convenient fiction.

But myth is not fiction: it consists of psychic facts that are endlessly repeated and can be sensed again and again, and whose resonances continuously influence mankind.

The fact that myths have been attributed to the life of Christ does nothing to disprove the psychic truth of his religio-spiritual value. Quite the contrary! I would even go so far as to say that, in positive terms, the inner mythical aspect of a life is precisely what expresses its universal human value.

And, on the negative side, it is also possible for the inner mythical aspects (in the shape of unconscious impulses or archetypes) to take complete possession of a man and overwhelm him and negatively impact his fate.

As well I know of instances where non-psychic, concrete phenomena have been generated by the subliminal power of an archetype.

The archetype fulfils itself not only subjectively in the individual, but objectively outside the individual. My own conjecture was that Christ was very much an archetypical persona.

The life of Christ is the life of God and a man at the same time. So Christ's persona is a bringing together of heterogenous natures, rather as if Job and Yahweh were combined in a single personality.

Yahweh's intention to become a man, which resulted from his collision with Job, is fulfilled in Christ's birth, life and sacrifice.

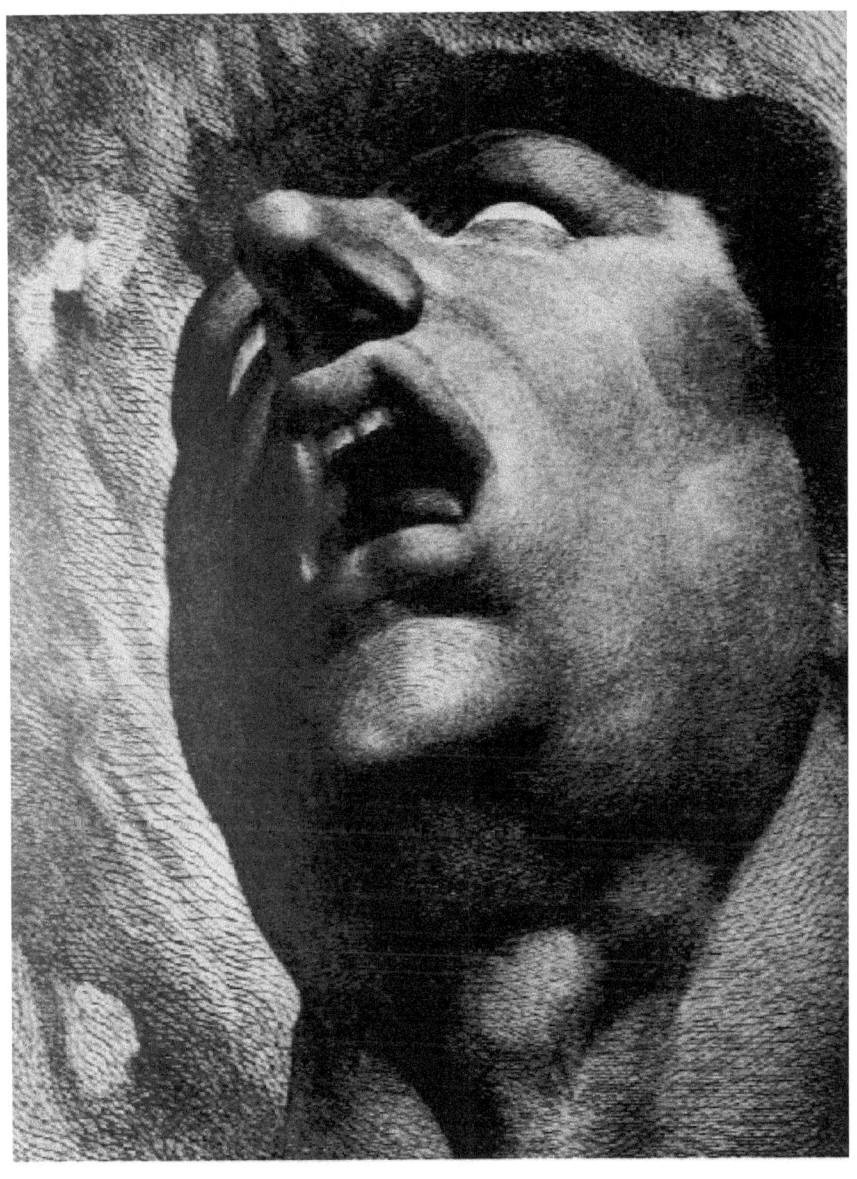

The way it used to be down below, old Testa style

The advent of Christ diminished Satan's power

I conjecture that Satan's comparative ineffectiveness after the advent of Christ can be demonstrated by the careful preparations for the divine birth, and later in adulthood by the curious metaphorical phenomenon that Christ witnessed: he saw Satan fall 'like lightning from heaven'.

In this 'lightning' vision, JC, by proffering an image of the metaphysical event, has sanctioned the historic and final separation of Yahweh from his dark son. Satan is banished from heaven and no longer has any opportunity to inveigle his father into malevolent undertakings. This event may well explain why he plays such a minor role wherever he appears after the Incarnation.

His role now is in no way comparable to his former confidential relationship to Yahweh. He has obviously forfeited the paternal complicity and is now exiled. The punishment which we missed in the story of Job has at last caught up with him, although in a strangely indirect form. Although he's banished from the heavenly court he has maintained some influence over the earthly world.

As a result of the partial neutralisation of Satan, Yahweh aligns with his light aspect and becomes the good God and loving father. He has not entirely lost his wrath and can still mete out punishment, but he does it with justice.

Cases like the Job trial are apparently no longer to be expected. He proves himself benevolent and gracious. The mercy he shows mercy to the sinful children of men is the manifestation of His love.

Satan with modish tatts being given the drill

> *JAN: Satan's role as the bad left hand of God has diminished, because in JC we have a totally 'good' son of God. Satan's role in preciptating the Job catharsis may have been the final straw that broke the camel's back, for which the treble outcome was the new son of God, a totally good God, and the depreciation of Satan's influence on men.*

The Demand hidden in the Lord's Prayer

But although Christ has confidence in his father, he cannot help inserting the cautious petition, nay, actually a demand and admonition into the Lord's prayer:

"Lead us not into temptation, but deliver us from evil."

The possibility that Yahweh, in spite of his express intention to become the **Summum Bonum**, *(the greatest good)* might yet revert to his former ways is not so remote as one might think. At any rate, Christ considers it appropriate to remind his father of his destructive inclinations towards mankind and to demand that he desist from them.

Judged by any human standards it is after all unfair, indeed extremely immoral, for an adsult to entice children into doing things that might be dangerous for them, simply in order to test their moral stamina! Especially as the difference between a child and an adult is immeasurably smaller than that between God and his creatures, whose moral weakness is particularly well-known to him.

I believe that the incongruity of it is so colossal that if this petition were not in the Lord's prayer, its existence anywhere else would be called a blasphemy of the highest order, because it really will not do ascribe such contradictory behaviour to the God of love and *Summum Bonum*.

WB in a Goya mode. Being a nice guy, this is rare

JAN: This is the killer insight in the book! CJ has fingered the text that proves his point. It is not an interpretation, but a written fact. 'Lead us not into temptation' is unlike any other line in the Lord's Prayer.

All the others like 'deliver us from evil' are requests, but 'lead us' is a demand loaded with eschatological implications. "If you are going to call yourself a just God, you can't play games with people and seduce them into doing bad things."

If one got nothing else out of the Answer to Job, this one insight would be enough to reconsider the nature of God, both Old and New!.. And....no ambivalent interpretations.... It's there in black and white!

Yahweh's moral defeat in his dealings with Job had its subliminal provocative effects: man's unintended elevation on the one hand, and on the other hand a disruption of God's Unconscious.

This inflames the uncon, which thereby acquires a higher moral 'pressure' than exists in consciousness.

In such situations the moral pressure starts flowing from the unconscious towards the conscious, in an anthropomorphic God as much as it does in man.

I have found that the Unconscious then erupts in the forms of dreams, visions and revelations. In God's case the eruption being God's revelatory insight that he needed to remake himself in the form of man - the ultimate apotheosis of anthropomorphic divinity.

God whirling around with a self composed vibe

> *JAN: For me Jung's analogy of 'flowing' conjures up an image of a Dali like flexible water tank that can absorb material up to the point when it becomes too full and overflows, spilling and wetting the areas around it... such analogies might provide imagery that would help comprehend such arcane and amorphous notions of the Conscious and Unconscious states.*

Post Book of Job and Pre Christ developments

In my understanding of the **Book of Ezekiel**, we meet for the first time the title 'Son of Man', which Yahweh significantly uses in addressing the prophet, presumably to indicate that he is the son of the 'Man' on the throne, and hence a prefiguration of the much later revelation in Christ.

Ezekiel grasped, if only in a symbolic fashion, the fact that Yahweh was drawing closer to man. This is something which may have come to Job as a vague feeling. Which would also mean that Job did not realise that his consciousness had become higher than Yahweh's. Gradually God became aware of this, so he was consequently drawn to becoming man.

This new measure of God's aroused Uncon gradually grew over the next few centuries. Around 165 BC, Daniel had a vision of four beasts and the 'Ancient of Days', to whom 'with the clouds of heaven there came one like a son of man'.

 Here the 'Son of Man' is not a prophet, but a son of the 'Ancient of Days' in his own right, and a son who is coming to rejuvenate the father.

Ezekiel looking improbably chilled out

> *JAN: Did Job figure out a lot more than he let on? CJ softly alludes to the possibility that Job had worked out that despite all the afflictions, he wasn't dead (or anywhere near it), and wasn't going to die because God wanted to keep him alive.... If so, it was all a game, a game in which it turned out that Job was better than God.... If Job knew this and played shtumm, then he was really, really smart....*

The book of **Enoch**, written around 100 BC, gives a quite compelling account of God's participation into the world of man. When Yahweh addressed Ezekiel as a 'Son of Man' it was no more than a dark and enigmatic hint. But with Enoch it becomes clear: the man Enoch is not only the recipient of divine revelation, but at the same time becomes a participant in the divine drama, as though he were almost one of the sons of God himself.

I gleaned that this means that in the same way in which God sets out to become man, man is also immersed in the **pleromatic** (*reverse divination*) process. Enoch is so much gripped by the influence of the divine that one could almost suppose he had a quite special understanding of the coming Incarnation.

The 'son of man' who is with the 'head' (or ancient) of days 'looks like an angel, that is like one of the sons of god. 'He hath righteousness'; 'With him dwelleth righteousness'; the lord of spirits has ' chosen him;' 'His lot hath the pre-eminence before the Lord of Spirits in uprightness.

It is remarkable that the 'son of man' and what he means should be associated again and again with righteousness. It seems to be his leitmotif, his chief concern. It is probably no accident that so much stress is placed on righteousness, which is the one quality that Yahweh lacks, a fact that I don't think could have remained hidden from such a man as the author of the book of Enoch.

Only where injustice threatens, does such an emphasis on righteousness make any sense. Only God can dispense justice to any noticeable degree, and man justifiably fears that God may forget his justice.

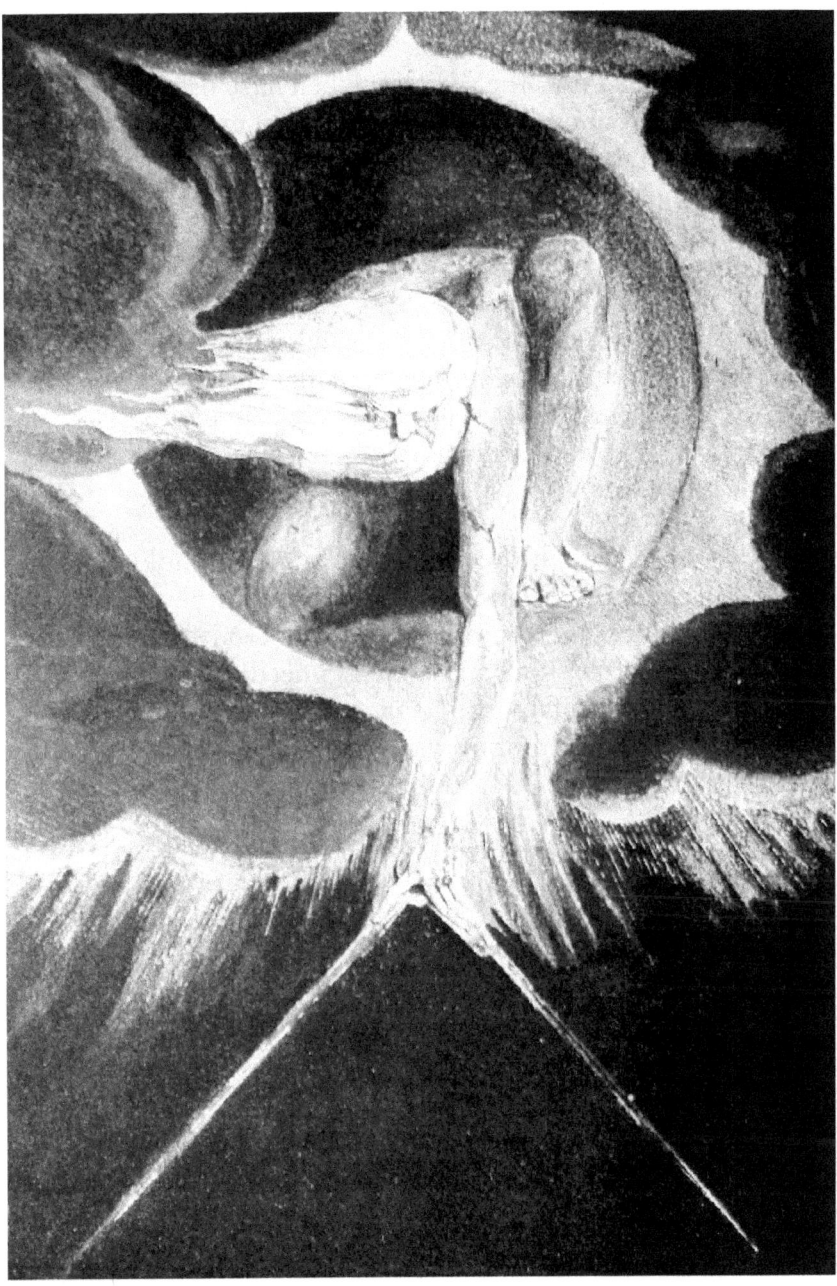

The Ancient of days. One of Blake's most famous images, the windy locks balancing out the architect of the universe theme

In the future Yahweh's righteous Son would intercede with him on man's behalf. Thus 'the righteous shall have peace'. That justice shall prevail under Jesus is stressed so much that one has the impression that under the reign of the father injustice was the norm, and that that true law and order only began with the advent of the Son. It looks like Enoch had unexpectedly given an answer to Job.

The emphasis laid on God's agedness (ancient of days) is relatively connected to the existence of the Son, but it also suggests to me that he himself will retreat a little into the background to leave the ruling of the human world more and more to the Son, in the hope that a more just order will emerge.

From this I can see the after effects of some psychological trauma, the memory of an injustice that cries to heaven and beclouds the intimate relationship between God and mankind. God himself wants a son, and man also needed God's son to take the place of his father. The son must be absolutely just, and this quality is given priority over all other virtues. God and man both want to escape from blind injustice.

Christ proves to be a mediator in two ways: he helps man against God and assuages the fear man feels towards this awesome being. He holds an important position midway between the two extremes, man and God. He is lacking neither in humanity nor in Divinity, and for this reason he was understood to unite both opposites. Christ by his descent, conception, and birth is a hero and half God in the classical sense.

He is virginally begotten by the Holy Ghost and, without sin, He encapsulates god's goodwill to the exclusion of all else.

Enoch, bearing a close family resemblance to Zeke, has eyes only for the heavenly task at hand.

God, with his good intentions, begot a 'light' son, Christ, and thus created an image of himself as the good father without admitting that there existed in him a very different dark truth.

Had he really been much more aware of himself, he would have seen what a profound disconnection he had provoked through his forthcoming incarnation. Where for instance, did his darkness go? That darkness, 'Satan', who always escapes punishment? After the birth does he think that he is completely changed and that his amorality has fallen away.

Why the crucifixion?

Christ offered himself as the expiatory sacrifice, as an act of grace that effects the reconciliation of God with mankind.

From a God who is a loving father one would expect understanding and forgiveness. So it comes as a nasty shock when this supposedly good God only allows the purchase of such an act of grace through a human sacrifice, and what is more, to the killing of his own son.

Christ apparently overlooked this violent incongruity and all theologians since have accepted it.

I believe that one of the greatest paradoxes in Christianity is that the God of goodness is so unforgiving that he can only be appeased by a human sacrifice, of a being without sin!

Be that as it may, Christ's unique sacrifice broke the curse of original sin and finally placated God.

His mates all come back offering gifts - standard father's day stuff, like hankies and socks

> *JAN: Another good insight from Carlo there! I have a couple of follow ups myself:*
>
> *Did God want his Son back as final ownership of his re-invention?*
>
> *Or wind back further: After Job's knowing of God, did God want to reinvent himself as an unknown modern divine being, and have him crucified, so JC would be taken away, and never be fully 'understood' by mankind? So, quite the difference from the premise that God desired/ needed consciousness!*
>
> *Instead of becoming totally conscious, did God precipitate the full Jesus episode to present a new aspect that would be fleeting and by its abrupt truncation could never be fully known?*

Conclusion

I posit that the inner instability of Yahweh is the prime cause not only of the creation of the world, but also initiates the divine drama for which mankind serves as a tragic witness and chorus. The encounter with the creature permanently changes the creator.

Yahweh's decision to become man resulted when He realised that man had became conscious of the entire God image - both good and bad. God was threatened by the unintentional Unconscious of Job (man), which forced him to harmonise with and unite the conflicting influences in his own mind.

God's unconscious wanted to merge with his conscious in order to reach completion, but until the testing of Job it consistently obstructed itself, because it would rather remain unconscious- blissfully unaware of itself. The Job cataclysm jolted God into a transformation- with a caveat. That is to say, God wanted to become man- because he desired man's new found wisdom, but not quite - he wanted to retain his innocence. This conflict in his nature was so great that the full Incarnation can only be brought by an expiatory self-sacrifice offered up to the wrath of God's dark side.

I conjecture that Job is the outward demonstration of God's Conscious/Unconscious dichotomy being resolved.

CARL JUNG 1938, SWITZERLAND.

Happy ending, and it was worth it, because Job and mankind learnt a lot

JOHN ANDREW NOBBS

Addendum :

How Jung's concepts inform the NSP

As I inferred in my introduction, I believe that the exercises we use in our actor training (the **Nobbs Suzuki Praxis**) have a lot of Jungian resonances. That is because we see performance as the modern equivalent of shamanistic societal completion. The actor as transformational shaman gives licence to the audience to have their own transformational experiences. For that modern actors require appropriate training.

Our training is a western variant of the original **Suzuki Method of Actor Training** (SMAT) developed by Japanese theatre director Tadashi Suzuki, who, for his profound and singular aesthetic, might be termed the Wagner/Kubrik of theatre.

Suzuki's training version is very spartan and terse, and I developed a strand which kept the core values of the original, but added improvisations more suited to the western actor.

The philosophy, routines, and tools evolved very instinctively, and only later as I read about Jung's work did I realise how much our exercises seemed to mirror so many Jungian precepts.

I admit to having only read Jung cursorily and scholars may well judge that I've got the wrong end of the stick, but it matters not a lot, as the exercises work very well, and certainly much better that all the others who keep to the Freudian side of the fence- which IMHO is all the rest!

The fundamental Jung takeaway is his notion of the two paradoxical sides of the mind; the Conscious and the Unconscious. Readers of this book would know by now what they stand for, but for my purposes, the Con deals with the 'facts' of life and the Uncon, the 'hows' and 'whys'.

Shamanistic acting is at its most compelling when the dialectics of self and role, good and bad, male and female, black and white, etc, are the foci of performance-and therefore the battleground of any training.

And it was astounding to me how well the NSP exercises were a serendipitous verification of Jungian 'Con/Uncon' dialectics.

The General Philosophy of the NSP

Knowledge and Mystery

Any performance is a dialectic between knowledge and mystery, from the micro of the actor's gesture to the macro of the entire aesthetic.

For example actors must have knowledge. i.e. the audience must trust that the actors have all the requisites to establish and sustain their 'journey' of the show.

This ranges from articulacy to stamina, and includes such prosaic factors as 'do they know when they are standing in the right light?'

But a performance must have a high degree of mystery. Otherwise it is a predictable display of a series of facts, such as the words and story- the sort of thing you'd get out of a book, and no reason to turn up at a live show. The mystery is the 'how'. How are the words are spoken, how does the story unfold?

The magical value that really defines an actor's performance is the mystery or charisma, that indefinable aura that can't be quantified beyond breathless epithets such as "Wow!" or "Marvelous!"

In Jungian terms, Con covers the Knowledge, and Uncon covers the Mystery, and any activity that makes performance compelling is governed by the Uncon- the personal Uncon of the actor connected umbilically with the personal and collective Unconscious of the spectators.

The attribute which most interferes with that connection between actor and audience is the Conscious minds of both.

For the actor the Conscious is the zone that hosts the destructive self criticisms such as "I'm not doing it right!... I wish I could be better, etc, etc". These are counter productive at best, and their presence can be disruptively felt by the observers.

On the other hand, if the actor's Conscious is trying to convince the audience by force of will, the conscious minds of the audience will gate keep: " I want what I want, not what you want me to accept!"

More successfully, if the actors are in an Uncon zone, where they are following some strand of personal mythology, it connects directly with the Uncon of the audience, both singular and collective, because the Unconscious does not gate keep. It continuously 'feels'.

Conscious daily behaviour within a performance setting becomes very predictable to watch. There's no revelation or surprise. The audience feels as if they already know what's going to happen. They're already on the beach waiting for the waves to break..

All great performers are successful because they 'live' in their Uncon zone on the stage. Most of them don't know they are doing it, and when asked will offer a very idirect answer: "Just feels like the right thing to do". Us plebs need to cultivate that zone, for which we need training.

When performers slip back into Conscious daily behaviour, the umbilical trust is be severed and the audience will start sliding into their own quotidian thinking: "Where can I get a coffee afterwards?"

Actors are always told they 'think' too much and that they should 'feel' more, which is true, but until Suzuki based training, there was no idiot proof solution. The simple answer is to stop the mind's 'thinking' (Conscious) from drowning out the mind's 'feeling' (Uncon). Easy to say, but harder to do!

There are two solutions.

One is to do activities where the Con relinquishes primacy because it is disconcerted by exhaustion and/or repetition - neither of which the Conscious can countenance.

The other solution is to get the Con to work with a clear realtime purpose e.g. actors are to continuously monitor their 'centre's' direct relationship with the floor as they proceed with a speech.

The Conscious 'thinking' being occupied by the clear mandate of the 'mechanics' frees up the Uncon to occupy and 'feel' its way through the creative field of the speech.

It may sound facile, but it does work, and it did work before I met Mr Jung, but his notions have made it that much easier to articulate the Hows and Whys of the process.

Primitive and Civilised

One of the questions surrounding performative shamanism in the Twenty First Century is: "How far do you go"? Back in the days of the method 'a la Lee Strasberg', quite a few actors went so far in the pursuit of 'emotional truth' that they never returned (another Freudian dry gully, methinks!).

At the time it might've seemed a good idea, but with all that collateral emotional wear and tear, its now known that such shamanising needs coralling.

We therefore developed a suite of exercises where the 'madness' is self-chaperoned, which is another way of saying that the Conscious mind creates a secure realm for the deep play of the Unconscious.

To ensure that the self chaperoning sustains, there is a clear outcome; a training speech must issue at the end of the routine, which means that throughout the 'madness', one part of the brain (the Conscious) is fully aware of an endgame (the speech). and that in fact, the 'madness' is both a preparation for the speech and its own separate experience.

No matter what the journey, it must also produce an output, and that output must perforce be a portrait of said journey.

The Con's purpose is to provide a sustaining safe space for the Uncon, means that the Con has relinquished its dominance, and has become a benevolent parent rather than a wilful participant.

Teddy Bears as Archetypes

We have used teddy bears in the training for quite some time, and they were introduced as a result of their involvement in a play I was directing for a group of 7 men, mostly beginners. At one stage I asked them to change the nappies on the teddy, whilst engaging in idle chit chat of the:

"My son's going to be a doctor/lawyer!" type badinage.

I was overwhelmed by the complete ease with which thay all performed the scene, and eventually put it down to the relationships with the teddys. Consequently, as well as introducing them as witnesses in all the other routines, I devised an exercise using Teds and found it very productive in revealing the actor's inner worlds,.

I came to the view that Teddy Bears represented for most people a return to their childhood age of innocence, before they 'knew' anything, with all the Proustian 'lost time' essence that former innocence implies. This seemed a very good Un Freudian way to generate 'memory recall' for compelling performance

I also believe that they initiate a type of access to an actor's personal mythology, which he can then learn to access, and cultivate.

Accessing one's personal mythology is a very Uncon thing to do, and it is very compelling to witness. One of the defining aspects of great performance is the private world of the actor being shared with the public world of the audience, and there is nothing more private than the actor's unique personal mythology.

We have taught the Teddy Bear exercise in many parts of the world, from Nepalese villages to hip young actor schools in the US, and have observed the same reactions from both male and female, old and young, etc, everywhere we've gone - that's surely an archetype!

BTW, since Jung was pretty keen on synchronicity, the Teddys are a good example, coming in to existence as toys in 1905 in both the USA and Austria with similar physiogomy, but quite independently and unknown to each other!

Self Interdiction

Another problematic issue for an actor is the accumulation of habitual speaking and moving. Problematic because, as I mentioned above, when an actor lapses into mannerisms the audience then drifts into quotidian thought patterns themselves.

Instead of being involved Unconsciously in the magical suspension of time and space of a shamanic event, their minds drift to daily 'chores' such as: "I wonder if I turned the oven off?"

This occurs for the actor when the actor's Conscious is dominating the experience, by interposing between the actor's self and the role that he is playing. This proclivity is quite human, but that doesn't make it any more productive.

Most acting nostrums attempt to drive around this domination by pretending the Conscious is not there: "Dont be nervous! Just relax!" Sort of a Freudian denial! Which for most people doesn't really work, because the Con really is present and cant be denied.

I'm sure CJ would have something to say about why this won't work.....

To prevent this interposition by the Conscious, we have developed advanced exercises where the actor, with a series of sharp sporadic physical interruptions, interdicts himself, preventing the 'turning on the auto pilot' and displaying predictable habits.

Some Con /Uncon tools

The image in the mirror is a myth.

We use hand held mirrors during any of the exercises at various times because it fosters a first and third person interdependence. As an actor sees himself in the mirror (held between 30 and 80 cms away), he has the sense of first person (I am) doing the exercise, as well as witnessing as a third person (he is) doing the exercise.

As well, if he's saying a speech looking at the mirror: he's talking to the mirror... he's watching himself talk to the mirror... he's talking to himself in the mirror etc. etc. His image in the mirror is not him, it's a copy of him.. it's a mythologised him, etc. etc...

At a point we face the mirror away, and still talking, remember the sensibility of the mythological image. This creates an actor who is both participant and witness.

Witness is the Conscious mind devolving from primary to secondary, and Participant is the un-fettered Uncon at deep play.

Holding the stick/holding onto the stick

The dialectic of the psyche's obverse and converse sides to enhance performing can be easily portrayed by a simple demonstration with a broomstick. I get the actor to hold the stick with both hands in a plain and undemanding position.

I then take hold of the stick and ask the actor to 'hold on to the stick', that is: let me take the entire weight of the stick, without letting the grip go completely slack.

Once I feel he has given me the entire weight, I then ask him to hold the stick as well as to be holding on to the stick... Both at the same time! This becomes a very profound experience for any performer! Of course one can extend the metaphor by saying: The stick is holding me...the stick is dancing me....etc. etc.

The facial features become more subtle and expressive, much more compelling than when actors are simply holding the stick. This is because they are now in 'dialogue' with the object, and that means that they are in a symbiotic physical 'conversation' with it.

This confers charisma on actors because of an aura surrounding them- their personal characters extend beyond their physical boundaries.

It may be argued that I am drawing a long bow equating mirrors and holding a stick, with Jung's Con /Uncon, but nevertheless the attitudinal shift in seeing the mind in Conscious and Unconscious terms triggers a multi layered sensibility for creating works of art.

For that I have to deeply thank Carl Jung, for his profound excavations of the human soul.

John Andrew Nobbs, Brissy, 2018

JOHN ANDREW NOBBS

www.ingramcontent.com/pod-product-compliance
Lightning Source LLC
Chambersburg PA
CBHW050112170426
43198CB00014B/2551